Family-Supportive Policies: The Corporate Decision-Making Process

by Dana E. Friedman

A Research Report from The Conference Board

Contents

Tables

Why This Report

There is growing recognition among corporate decision makers that changes in the American family are affecting recruitment efforts, benefit plans, productivity incentives and, ultimately, the bottom line. These shifts pose two challenges to business leaders: first, *whether to respond* to their employees' family concerns; and second, *how to respond* in ways that serve the organization as well as the employee.

The Work and Family Information Center, The Conference Board's clearinghouse on corporate policies that concern the family, is frequently asked about these issues by Associate firms. This report describes the information gathered by more than 75 leading-edge companies in the emerging field of work and family life. Its purpose is to help managers as they decide whether and how to conduct their own fact finding on this challenging issue.

This research indicates that the tasks of assessing the relationship between work and family life and developing appropriate policies and practices for the company are far more complicated than most executives anticipate. Many of the companies interviewed for this report spent more than two years contemplating involvement and investigating their options. Company task forces reviewed research, observed other firms' programs, surveyed managers and employees, and assessed community resources before making recommendations. We are grateful to all the executives who shared their company's decision-making strategies so that others might benefit from their experience.

JAMES T. MILLS
President

METHODOLOGY

This report reflects interviews in 15 cities with more than 75 companies and 50 community organizations that work with the private sector. Those interviewed included company executives responsible for planning or administering family-support initiatives, as well as service providers, researchers, government officials, and other community leaders involved with creating new programs and policies to assist working families. Additional contacts were made with Conference Board Associates when the staff of the Work and Family Information Center were asked to offer individual company consultation to 15 company task forces focusing on work and family concerns. Ongoing contact with these task forces provided a longitudinal view of their research efforts. Because the decision-making process is usually lengthy, only a few of these task forces have implemented recommended solutions at this writing. Finally, contacts with consultants, employed by companies to investigate employer-supported child care, also provided valuable input.

Chapter 1
Introduction

Most managers devise organizational strategies based on the common-sense assumption that decision making is a rational process. Sometimes, however, the politics and culture of an organization foil even the most "rational" of plans.

One management consultant contends that "when well-managed major organizations make significant changes in strategy, the approaches they use frequently bear little resemblance to the rational analytical systems so often described in the planning literature."[1] Other observers believe that blind reliance on rational managerial approaches is one reason U.S. business has lost its competitive edge.[2]

These comments are not meant to suggest a loss of faith in rationality; but rather, they are an acceptance of its limits. A rational approach, executives contend, requires that all options be weighed and judgments be based on merit. But this view ignores the reality that most decisions are inherently political and that personal and political factors will always play a role.

Another assumption is that the rational approach can produce decisions quickly and efficiently. Yet, in most cases where significant change is required, considerable time is spent garnering suppport for new ideas. A Chase Manhattan Bank vice president comments: "One of the biggest liabilities of the rational model is that it doesn't help managers recognize that the change represented by a major decision is almost always resisted and prolonged resistance is much of what makes decision processes inordinately inefficient." This is particularly true when decisions relate to family issues at the workplace.

Any change may be resisted because of an organization's culture.[3] When changes are proposed on issues related directly to work and family concerns, resistance can become passionate. Many managers do not believe that family issues are an "appropriate" business concern. Thus, the legitimacy of the topic is resisted, even before any specific suggestions have been made or recommendations for change have been proposed.

Some claim that the traditional denial of any connection between family and work is due to an earlier "overinvolvement" on the part of some companies in the lives of their employees. During a brief period around the turn of the century, companies not only concerned themselves with their employees, but also tried to control them in paternalistic fashion. For example, some sent inspectors into employees' homes to make sure they were adequate and respectable.

Others conclude that the traditional separation of work and family was necessary for the smooth and efficient functioning of each. The belief was that their respective standards were inherently in conflict: Where the family acted on mores, values and emotion, the corporation was said to be motivated by more objective criteria. As long as the division of labor maintained women at home and men at work, this argument was difficult to contradict. In recent years, traditional sex roles have blurred, and so has the line between work and family life.

Another reason why companies might have minimized— or ignored— family issues is that many managers have not been trained to look at non-work factors as having any bearing on work performance. Much of the classical organizational research was conducted before the major influx of women into the labor force and many of management's prevailing theories were developed from research on male workers in the 1950's.

Finally, some managers may resist addressing work and family issues among workers because they fear involvement in the personal lives of employees. They justify such fears on the basis of public outrage over governmental interference in personal lives and predict that such criticism will shift to the private sector.

Such corporate attitudes and values are often raised when issues of family life are discussed. Some contend that this view may be affected by the life styles of people in decision-making roles. The executives interviewed agreed that the vast majority of today's top-echelon decision makers have not had to grapple with the difficulties of balancing work and

[1] James Bryant Quinn, "Formulating Strategy One Step at a Time." *Journal of Business Strategy*, Winter, 1981, p. 43.

[2] See, for example, Thomas J. Peters and Robert H. Waterman, Jr., *In Search of Excellence: Lessons from America's Best-Run Companies.* New York: Harper and Row, 1982, Chapter 1 and 2.

[3] See Melissa Berman, *Corporate Culture and Change: Highlights of a Conference.* The Conference Board, Report No. 888, 1986.

...ecutives—overwhelming-
...e tending to the children and
...suggested that company con-
...g for aging relatives may increase
...makers are more likely to have
...hoolers.[4] Without this personal ex-
...ly issues are often considered primarily u... ...their effect on the organization's
self-intere... ...ttom-line performance.

Overcoming Resistance

Some organizational scholars believe that companies will become more responsive to family issues when there is significant "pain," that is, when family-related problems cause management concern. As one researcher points out: "If there is one thing of which researchers are very certain, it is that organizations do change when they are under pressure and rarely when they are not."[5]

For this reason, the most successful strategies for overcoming resistance to considering work and family issues have been to define the issues as broadly as possible, making them relevant to the variety of internal and external forces that exert pressure on the organization. All of the companies interviewed were able to identify at least one of the factors listed below as having provided the motivation for their concern about the family needs of workers:

- Facing a demand for labor, the company decides to provide family benefits in order to help recruit skilled workers.
- Concerned about both foreign and domestic competition, the company hopes that easing work-family conflicts will result in a more productive work force.
- Absenteeism and tardiness might be reduced, a company decides, if working parents had more stable child-care arrangements.
- Management accepts the popular criticism of business as ignoring its "human resources" and tries to become more people oriented and participatory in its management style.
- Concerned about its image in the community, the company pursues "partnerships" with local government and service agencies in order to provide needed family support services.
- Faced with the "pyramid squeeze" (increased competition for top positions from well-qualified members of the baby-boom generation), the company compensates otherwise deserving individuals by providing more family-supportive benefits.

- Pressure from a womens' advocacy organizations stimulates discussion in the company on ways to provide more support to women as they move up the management ladder.
- The company finds that the worker, around whom benefits and work schedules were originally designed, is no longer typical. The demographics of the labor force are seen to have made many long-standing company policies obsolete and ineffective.

Defining work and family issues in terms of corporate self-interest helps connect the decision-making process to longer-term, broad-based corporate change and its legitimacy as a business issue is better established. (See box.)

Defining the Problem

For many corporations, child-care needs emerge before most other family-related concerns. Thus, many firms' task forces organized to examine family needs began as the "Company X Child Care Task Force." Our research shows that most companies that began by focusing on child-care issues eventually enlarged the scope of their inquiry—and the name of their task force—to "work and family" concerns. This change occurred because organizers recognized the desirability of gaining a broad corporate constituency. While firms' original concerns might be for working parents, the focus soon expanded to include other employees—for example, those who might be having problems with approaching retirement, an older parent, or a handicapped dependent.

It is often assumed that work and family problems are primarily "women's problems." But the company managers interviewed repeatedly cautioned against this narrow view. They observed that the changing demographics have caused men to become increasingly involved with family and child-care matters. Research also suggests that when men take on more family responsibilities, they begin to experience the same strains as women. While women take on more tasks, men are not immune to the negative effects of the dual responsibilities for home and work.[6]

Managers also argued that the issue tends to become more threatening and emotional when defined solely as a woman's problem. Some report that their male allies are critical during the research process. Excluding men from the debate, they say, is self-defeating for it is largely men who occupy the higher echelons of management and who will be responsible for final decision making. Another reason for beginning with a broad definition of work family issues is to gain the flexibility needed to deal with the unexpected. Thus, even if an unexpected dimension of work-family conflict is identified, it is likely to fall within the purview of the approved research effort.

[4] See Dana Friedman, "Eldercare: The Employee Benefit of the 1990's," *Across the Board*, June, 1986, pp. 45-51.

[5] Michael Beer, *Organization Change and Development: A Systems View.* Santa Monica, Louisiana: Goodyear Publishing Company Inc., 1980, p. 48.

[6] Dianne S. Burden and Bradley Googins, *Balancing Job and Homelife Study: Summary of Research Findings.* Boston: Boston University School of Social Work, 1985.

Defining the Solution

Many of the companies interviewed say that the first time they heard about family needs of workers was when an employee suggested that the company build an on-site day-care center. In a typical case, a group of employees then examined the feasibility of establishing such a program. In most cases they decided against the idea. In fact, some reported, if anything has discouraged companies from responding to family issues, it is the misconception that the only solution is to build a day-care center.

A Variety of Corporate Self-Interests[1]

The diversity of rationales for company involvement in child care can be illustrated by the twelve companies that jointly sponsored the Quality Child Care System, a child-care referral and training program in Holland, Michigan. When asked what factors influenced their company's decision to participate in this program, company representatives responded as follows:

"There are two reasons why we're involved in this program. The first is a selfish one. We realized that we had the potential of losing skilled people because of their child-care problems. Parents sometimes find conflicts between their parenting responsibilities and their work responsibilities. Then, secondly, we saw this as a challenge to the private sector to pick up the slack by providing financial support to a community agency that was helping parents find solutions to their child-care needs."
Vice President, J.W. Brooks Enterprises, Inc.

"We are interested in improving the quality of life for employees. This program came along at a good time. We believe it will help reduce absenteeism and turnover, even reduce stress for employees."
Vice President, Bil Mar Foods, Inc.

"The opportunity to help employees by providing this child-care service as a benefit was looked on by the company as a good business decision. We recognized that participation in this joint venture added to a good public image."
Personnel Manager, BLD Products Ltd.

"Our company has a philosophy of wanting to make life as comfortable as we can for employees. A child-care service is what would be expected considering this philosophy."
Personnel Coordinator, Bradford Company

"We didn't feel that we had the resources to provide direct child care to our employees, so helping to fund a community-coordinated child-care referral agency was a timely opportunity to help ourselves and our employees. Quality child care is no longer just a concern of parents; it's a major concern to all of us. Child-care problems for working parents often translate into problems in the workplace, and working parents form a major part of our employee population. As a bottom-line issue, child care is a good, sound business decision."
Personnel Director, Donnelly Corporation

"Haworth looks for a payback from the Quality Child Care System program. We believe that working parents who have good care for their children are likely to be more productive than those who have a lot of child-care problems."
Member Services Representative, Haworth, Inc.

"The Quality Child Care System gives us the opportunity to respond to employees' needs for child-care assistance without the expense of time required of the other employer-sponsored child-care alternatives. The sponsoring group, 4C, a child advocate agency, is doing what it does best, letting us concentrate on what we do best."
Director of Human Resources, Herman Miller, Inc.

"The information and referral service has been helpful to employees, particularly newcomers to town. The service creates the sense that there is some sort of quality control."
Personnel Director, Holland Hospital

"When I'm interviewing a young parent who is reentering the workforce, in eight out of ten interviews the question comes up: 'Can you give me any suggestions on where to find child care?' The program gives me a good source of information to help them answer that question."
President of Manpower Temporary Services

"ODL has a philosophy of honest concern for employees. The child-care resource and referral service is a benefit that we can offer employees that is cost effective."
Personnel Director, ODL

"Participation in the program was recognized as good public relations and helped to create a good community image."
Personnel Director, Parke-Davis

"Being part of the QCCS is good publicity. We are listed as a participant among companies that care about children. The cost is nominal compared to the benefit of just knowing our employees have this help available."
Personnel Director, Trendway Corporation

[1] Bonnie Church Piller, *Holland Area Employer- Sponsored Community Coordinated Child Care: A Case Study*. Unpublished dissertation, Western Michigan University, August 1985 pp. 128-129.

While the establishment of a day-care center may prove to be the most appropriate response, managers emphasize that other objectives are achieved by investigating the full range of solutions. One of the explanations for the growth in employer-supported child care has been the education provided to companies about the alternatives to on-site child care. When compared to several alternatives, the final choice is more easily justified and management receives a more thorough education about ways in which the work environment can be made more sensitive to the family needs of workers.

Sick-leave policies, work schedules, or even production quotas might be causing strains that companies want to eliminate. A more extensive exploration into a range of company policies and practices can help management focus on those that can create work-family conflict. The managers point out that while the obvious temptation is to design innovative new benefits and services, firms might achieve just as much by modifying—or abandoning—existing policies and practices found to be counterproductive. The accompanying box illustrates a broad range of issues and program solutions that work and family task forces often assess.

Work and Family Solutions

Creating or Supporting Child-Care Services
- On-or near-site day-care center
- Consortium child-care center
- Network of family day-care homes
- Before- and after-school programs
- "Warm lines" for school-age children[1]
- Summer day camp
- Sick child-care infirmary
- In-home nursing service for sick children

Providing Counseling and Referral Services
- Employee-assistance programs with family counseling
- In-house referral service for child care or eldercare
- Contract with community resource and referral agency or case-management service
- Family education seminars
- Community-service fairs at the workplace

Offering Financial Assistance
- Discounts at local community programs
- Voucher (direct subsidy) programs
- Comprehensive cafeteria plans with a dependent-care assistance plan[2]
- Flexible spending account with salary reduction for dependent care
- Adoption benefits
- Tuition assistance for children's college

Easing Time Constraints
- Flexitime
- Part-time work
- Job sharing
- Summer hours
- Work at home
- Sick child-care leave
- Extended maternity and paternity leave
- Parental leave, including adoptive parents
- Personal family leave
- Social service leave to aid community organizations

Donating to Community Services
- Corporate contributions to local programs
- Corporate support for community projects of employees' family members
- In-kind donations of space, time
- Start-up loan funds
- Investment in training of community agency staff to improve quality
- Lobbying on legislative issues

Accommodating Major Transitions
- Relocation and counseling assistance
- Family-support services after work-force reductions or plant closings
- Pre-retirement counseling

[1] Warm lines are "nurturing hotlines."
[2] Dependent care includes care of children, older parents and handicapped dependents.

Chapter 2
Organizing the Company's Research Effort on the Work-Family Interface

The design of a corporate response to employees' family concerns ultimately depends upon a unique blend of (l) management goals, (2) employee needs, and (3) community resources. This report describes the strategies that can produce needed information about these three ingredients of decision making. Companies report, however, that preliminary research is often necessary before embarking on a thorough investigation of these factors. The purposes of preliminary research are to:

(1) Assess the firm's internal environment—specifically, management receptivity to family issues and organizational resources.
(2) Substantiate the need for further investigation based on work-force demographics, activities among competitors and the experiences of those employers already providing family support.
(3) Determine the scope and direction of further research.

Preliminary research involves an environmental scan of internal and external attitudes and resources. Some facets of this research might be investigated as part of the more formal, comprehensive research effort; some might not be necessary at all. The experiences of several corporations indicate that the search for specific data and its place in the research process will vary, depending on the level of support within the company for addressing family issues at the workplace. The greater the support from the top, the less research that is needed.

Internal Environment

Executives in companies that have responded to the family needs of their employees recommend having a well-formulated strategy that can marshal and allocate an organization's resources. The strategy is ultimately based upon the company's competencies and shortcomings, the anticipated changes in the environment, and likely areas of resistance.[1] Such a strategy commands, "know thyself." It requires information about:

- corporate readiness for addressing family concerns
- the level of management support
- the financial and managerial resources of the organization
- the structure and unique characteristics of the organization
- the potential return on investment (as discussed in Chapter 6).

Corporate Readiness

Corporate readiness can depend on the organization's view of family issues as a legitimate business concern and the timing of the proposal. If the company just experienced downsizing, for instance, job-placement activities are likely to take precedence over family concerns.[2] On the other hand the company might recognize the personal stress associated with layoffs and make a special effort to address family concerns. Management may also be less willing to experiment with new services after a previous failure. For years, AT&T was said to hold a negative view of child-care provision because of a failed experiment in the early 1970's. Fifteen years later, it seems ready to investigate a new solution.

Management Support

Management support for an investigation of work and family issues might come in the form of a mandate originating at the top of the firm, a sanctioning of a bottom-up initiative, or a shared responsibility among various levels of employees. The level of management support needed depends, of course, on the structure of the organization, the degree of centralization, and on the firm's previous commitments to family issues.

Top-management's involvement helps in the identification of talented people in the organization who can contribute to the research effort. A top manager may know of others who have expressed an interest in the subject, and decision makers who are likely to be sympathetic to the issues.

---

[1] James Bryant Quinn, 1981, pp. 42-63.

[2] See Ronald Berenbeim, *The Impact of Plant Closings*. The Conference Board, Report No. 878, 1986.

Even though management may be willing to support the initial research effort, respondents warn that this does not guarantee later acceptance of proposed recommendations. Sometimes, they say, circumstances may change, apathy sets in, and new problems arise that overshadow this issue. Thus, the research, executives say, should be accompanied by an educational effort to dispel family-issue stereotypes, and, in the process, management should be prepared for the findings and eventual recommendations to come.

Resources of the Organization

Internal resources of the organization can often be used to enrich the research effort. For example, Procter & Gamble's experience in consumer behavior and market research was helpful in conducting a thorough exploration of child-care options. A toy company that has a testing center, where children play with new products, had the staff and some of the information necessary for evaluating a child-care center for employees.

Employee Attitudes

While exceptionally rare, there have been instances in which the employees felt that they did not want the company to be involved in any way in their personal lives. One Minnesota company reports that employees rejected a plan to investigate an on-site child-care center, fearing an overinvolvement by the company in their family affairs. Employees may also resist company counseling programs because of a concern about confidentiality.[3]

Structure and Characteristics of the Organization

Some companies have unique features that affect the scope of the research effort and the range of possible solutions. For example, a company with fewer than 100 employees, in several locations, would probably not be interested in establishing an on-site day-care center—except in a consortium with other small employers. A unionized company might seek the participation of labor at some point in the research process: The timing of the research might be coordinated with contract negotiations.

Organizational information is also important for later comparisons with other companies. Many of the companies interviewed underscored the need to be aware of differences between one's own company and those of another firm whose family-support program is being examined or borrowed. Substantial modifications might be necessary before such a program can be transplanted.

External Environment

Managers find that the practices of other companies, government policies, the attitudes of the public, and demographic trends have important relevance for a company's behavior. Beyond the obvious substantive insights this information can provide, an examination of the external environment can also help to identify individuals who can provide needed expertise for further research.

Competitor Companies

Most companies measure themselves against their competitors. As Amory Houghton, retired chairman of the board of Corning Glass Works, has said: "One percent of all companies want to be first and 99 percent want to be second."[4] The experiences of the pioneering one percent may be instructional—and inspirational—when designing or implementing new programs.

Most companies begin with a state-of-the-art review of other company programs. A secondary analysis highlights programs in those companies that are more similar to their own. The criteria used for "borrowing"— or replicating— another company's program include such factors as: industry, region, locations, number of employees, degree of unionization, and corporate culture. Industry size and type are critical for major competitors. For example, Johnson and Johnson conducted a survey of 55 companies in the pharmaceutical industry to learn about their family-support initiatives before initiating its own program. The Council on Financial Competition conducted a study of bank programs for working mothers. The Council then distributed a series of brief case studies to its member institutions.

Smaller companies in the same communities rely on the same labor pool and must remain competitive. Competition among firms can spill over into the public sector. For instance, several state capitals reported that the growth of private industry placed state government in competition for labor with the private sector. As a result, state agencies are considering a range of child-care and family benefits as a way to establish a recruitment edge.

Because corporate responses to family needs are often shaped by the supply of services in the community, as well as the family demographics of the region, managers say it is important to weigh these conditions when considering another company's program. The success of that program might depend on a particular configuration of families or the sophisticated delivery system of family-support services. An extended family, for example, is more common in the South and relatives may be able to provide a greater amount of child-care support. In the early 1970's, Levi Strauss & Company learned this lesson after an on-site center in Arkansas failed due to underutilization. Parents in that area preferred the less costly part-time care provided by relatives.

In California, BankAmerica has instituted a child-care provider recruitment and training program that is largely pos-

[3] Helen Axel (Ed.), *Corporate Strategies for Controlling Substance Abuse*, The Conference Board, Report No. 883, 1986.

[4] Amory Houghton, speech presented at national conference on "New Management Initiatives for Working Parents," sponsored by Boston University School of Management and Wheelock College. Boston, Massachusetts: April 2, 1981.

sible because of the existence of the statewide system of resource and referral agencies. Elements of the bank's program can be borrowed, but the system may not be easily replicated elsewhere due to the lack of funding for child-care referral services in other states.

One of the most important observations to make when examining the family initiatives of other companies, managers say, is the culture in which it was born. A unique corporate environment may be the reason for the program's success. A particularly innovative solution may be an indication of strong, companywide support for the program. Without a similar commitment, the program might be underutilized elsewhere. Employee use of child-care resource and referral (R & R) services varies among companies that contract for these services. In one Boston company, the R & R contract was established after a one-year investigation by a company task force. A nearby competitor learned of the program and arranged for a similar contract. But the second employer did not have the same level of commitment to the program and spent considerably less time informing employees about the program. The utilization rate for employees of this company was 75 percent less than that of the first firm's.

Visits

The executives interviewed believe it is worthwhile to visit those companies whose programs are under serious consideration. With regard to day-care centers, it is often more valuable to examine the salaries, fees and quality of centers in the same community—even those without corporate sponsorship—since parents will be faced with a choice between the company program and the regular supply of services. It is also helpful to visit the programs sponsored by companies in other parts of the country that have received a great deal of press coverage.

One New Jersey training and consulting firm gives tours of the on-site centers in New Jersey and Pennsylvania. A unique opportunity exists in this area for executives to talk to managers in companies and to visit programs that represent the full range of administrative structures for establishing a day-care center. This day-and-a-half tour includes six day-care centers and visits with center directors and company managers responsible for their creation.

Some companies have made it easy for others to learn about their programs. IBM and BankAmerica have prepared literature or shared information on their counseling and child-care initiatives. The child-care center of American Savings and Loan (in Irvine, California) is described in a videotape that the company is willing to share. Most of the companies with flexible benefits have booklets for employees that are also useful to other companies. Stride Rite Children's Centers sponsor meetings in conjunction with the Child Care Resource Center of Cambridge, Massachusetts, for employers interested in visiting the company's two day-care centers and learning about their operation. Wang Labs, Steelcase,

Inc., and Corning Glass Works have sponsored conferences to educate other employers about a range of child-care options and to highlight their own successes.

Public Attitudes

Recognizing the novelty and sensitivity of corporate attention to family issues, executives often consider the attitudes of the surrounding community before pursuing such involvement. For example, one corporation, with operations in a relatively conservative state, was concerned about the potential for a public backlash after announcing its plans for a child-care program. After discovering the absence of state or national data measuring public attitudes toward child care, this company, along with several other corporations, is considering funding such a study on community attitudes toward child-care services.

Government Activity

There may be new programs developed with public funding that provide opportunities or incentives for company involvement. Bills before state legislatures, if enacted, may require a forced response by corporations. The timing of legislative activities has significant implications for companies, as recent legislative and regulatory debates on flexible benefits have shown. An increasing number of companies are reviewing their parental leave policies as Congress debates the merits of various bills that would mandate such leave.

Experts in the Community

Relatively impartial surveyors of local services, such as United Way staff, university researchers and government personnel can provide a window on the supply, demand and quality of family services in the community. They can also direct employees to appropriate consultants and to high-quality service providers. During the initial stage of research, it is useful to identify the most competent individuals who can later describe the strengths and weaknesses of community-based services.

Some of the companies studied stopped their investigations after conducting preliminary research. They might have found little evidence of industry activity, or they were not convinced that family issues are a major concern among their employees. Several companies chose to wait until business improved or another, more pressing, problem was solved.

Most companies, however, proceed with a more intensive research effort. The responsibility for further research might be given to one individual in the organization or to a group of employees organized into a task force.

The Written Plan or Proposal

Several companies require the submission of a written proposal to conduct further research. A written plan is useful, even if not required, in order to conceptualize the goals and the process, to establish lines of authority, and to assign responsibilities among those working together.

The written plan also demonstrates the seriousness of the task to be undertaken. Other corporate initiatives require written documentation and a plan of action. Since the subject of work and family life might be perceived as "soft" by some, the managers say an exploration of work and family issues should follow the same practices applied to "hard" issues considered by the business organization. The written document typically includes:

- statement of purpose
- areas of investigation
- responsibilities of various staff
- anticipated outcomes
- cost of the investigation
- time frame

Hiring Consultants

Author Robert Townsend, of *Up the Organization* fame, questioned the integrity of consultants, saying: "They borrow your watch to tell you what time it is and then walk off with it."[5] But despite what skepticism might accompany the hiring of consultants, nearly every company researching its response to family needs has hired a consultant. Most firms find the subject of family issues at the workplace to be sufficiently complex to believe that it would be more efficient to hire an experienced outsider, rather than to try to master the

[5] Robert Townsend, *Up the Organization.* New York: Alfred A. Knopf, 1970, p. 104.

subject in-house. Consultants were also thought to shorten the research process and reduce the work load for company personnel.

Most managers felt that the most valid reason to call in outside expertise is to gain the "best thinking" on the subject, in the hope that such knowledge can prevent the company from repeating the mistakes of other companies. And, hopefully, the consultant can steer the company toward some of the more successful strategies of other companies. (See box for an example.)

The consultant can provide the names of managers in other companies who have already been through the decision-making process. They can also direct the manager in charge of the investigation to research studies, newspaper articles, and other sources of information as well as help to prepare background materials for the company.

An outsider may also be helpful in smoothing relations with employees and the community. In a small bank outside Boston, the consultant responsible for analyzing an employee survey hand-delivered the surveys to each employee. The bank wanted to make sure that the employees knew that the information was not going to be reviewed by bank managers, but by a consultant. Employees were told to direct all questions about the survey to this consultant.

Consultants may also have a collegial relationship with (or understanding of) service providers and government officials. As a result, they may be able to produce more efficient and insightful evaluations of community resources than

---

Consultation Services for Arlington County, Virginia's Government Task Force on Child Care

A Child Care Task Force was appointed in December, 1982, to determine an appropriate response for the county government to make to the childcare needs of its employees. The task force comprised a cross-section of employees, who brought the issue to the attention of management during a discussion of future compensation proposals. The task force first met on January 12, 1983, and met on a bi-weekly schedule. Members reviewed factors influencing costs, support services, funding, services for children with special needs, and local child-care operations. They also conducted a survey of all permanent employees. Their work was scheduled for completion by July, 1983. In May of 1983, a consultant was hired to help the task force analyze the collected data.

An outline of the consultant's services is presented below:

I Review data collected
  A. Sort data
  B. Point out critical things overlooked
  C. Discard non-critical data
  D. Suggest how data should be used
II Assess survey data
  A. Evaluate employee needs assessment survey data

  B. Recommend other surveys, if needed, and design questionnaire
III Recommend methodologies
  A. Review goals of the task force and revise, if necessary
  B. Review future work plans
  C. Guide the development of assumptions
  D. Guide the development of conclusions
  E. Provide general cost estimates of alternatives
IV Facilitate discussion
  A. Attend two or three task force meetings to facilitate discussions within the study group
  B. Attend other meetings, as necessary
V Evaluate the final task force report

The results of this effort led the task force to propose the creation of an on-site child-care center and administrative policy changes to support employees with dependents. Many of the recommendations have been adopted, such as flexitime and expanded opportunities for part-time employment with the county. Efforts are underway to identify a suitable site for a child-care center that will serve county employees and residents.

---

would a corporate manager unaware of local resources. Sometimes a consultant from outside the community is appropriate for making an objective assessment of local providers.

When to Hire a Consultant

Deciding whether to acquire outside expertise will depend on the company's tendency to hire external consultants, the level of expertise inside the company, and available funding to pay for consultation. Managers say a consultant might be hired at the times of:

- design of the research investigation
- employee needs assessment
- community assessment
- selecting a company response
- implementation of programs
- evaluation of programs

Most often, consultants are hired at the very beginning of the research process. The consultant's role is to help structure the investigation, often beginning with the design and analysis of an employee questionnaire. In some instances, depending on the company's chosen couse of action, a consultant different than the one hired for initial research might be hired to help design or implement a program. For instance, the work and family expert might not be knowledgeable about implementing a flexitime program. A different area of knowledge might also be required during the evaluation phase. In this case, general research skills may be more important than a specialized knowledge of work and family issues.

In practice, companies often rely on more than one consultant. They may have one individual shepherding them through the overall process, while relying on others to provide specialized expertise. Staff from the Work and Family Information Center of The Conference Board often provide one-day consultations to company task forces. The Center is called upon to provide an overview of national trends, the range of family-support initiatives, and descriptions of the most successful practices in the area of work and family programming.

Consultants' Skills

What most companies described, when asked about the kind of person they looked for as a consultant on work and family issues, was someone who was "bilingual"—albeit not in the traditional sense of the term. Ideally, they want someone who understood the needs of parents and the community, but who was also conversant with the language of management and knowledgable about the competing pressures on a business organization. Sensitivity to management's needs can make for a better working relationship and help to produce a set of recommendations more compatible with the culture and goals of the organization.

Many work and family consultants are former providers of service or researchers—some of whom may have a continuing stake in the program's outcome. The consultant selected should be familiar with the service delivery system as well as with broad policy concerns affecting the system's administration and funding.

How Companies Select a Consultant

Many companies called their colleagues in other companies (where they knew similar research had already been conducted) to find recommended consultants. The local Chamber of Commerce, United Way, or child-care referral service are also sources. In several company investigations of family needs, the spouse of a task-force member was in the field of child care and provided needed consultation. Grants to local communities from the federal and state governments have enabled local community-based organizations to develop a consulting capacity. Oftentimes, such consultants are provided at low or no cost.

With the considerable media attention on the subject, newspaper and magazine articles also prove useful in identifying consultants. National organizations involved in work and family programs typically have local networks that can be tapped.

Several companies mentioned that "compatibility" was important in the hiring of consultants. When asked why they hired a specific consultant they remark: "We get along well." Another commented: "I sensed that we could have a productive work relationship as well as some fun."

One of the most important criteria for hiring consultants, as mentioned by several companies, was how "well-connected" they were to other sources of professional expertise. Even though the company might have their own tax experts, accountants and organizational development specialists, the area of work and family may be so specialized that outside help might be needed at some point to round out the knowledge of the consultant. For this reason, several consultants in this field have "advisory boards," or connections with individuals with such skills. Companies appreciate consultants who are astute enough to extend their consulting base.

How Much Do They Cost?

In the child-care field, some companies assumed that a consultant's services, if obtained from a public service agency or nonprofit institution should be rendered free of charge. But consultant fees are an essential source of revenues in a growing number of organizations.

As mentioned earlier, there are instances where the state provides funding to a local agency to conduct a family-needs assessment. One company commented: "We wouldn't have been able to afford to assess our employees' needs without their free consultation." However, an executive at another company commented: "I know that we were the beneficiaries of the state's goodwill but, frankly, I think that my tax dollars could be better spent. This is the kind of cost that our company should pay. After all, we pay people to come in and teach us how to write memos. Why not for eldercare or child care?"

One other way to obtain some free consultation is to include members of the outside community on the company task force. ARCO Alaska, Inc. included on its task force the director of child-care services for the State's Department of Social Services, a licensing official from the city, and the leader of the community college, who has been active in the communitywide task force on work and family issues.

Chapter 3
Forming Task Forces

In most of the companies interviewed it was possible to identify one individual who was a catalyst in awakening company concern for family issues. Typically, soon after this "awakening" management appointed a team of employees to gather the research necessary for decision making. Visits with a number of these task forces show that several benefits accrue to the employees who participate in them. The primary ones are:

- a shared work load
- an increased pool of expertise
- a broadening of internal political support

Individual task force members praised the team approach for reasons that often went beyond the feelings of satisfaction derived from their contribution. To begin with, team members were grateful for the opportunity to collaborate with their co-workers and learn more about their employers. Most felt that through the task force they learned as much about the policies and culture of the organization as they did about work and family issues.

Managers recommended two ingredients for the success of a task force's deliberations:

1) *Top management commitment*, without which, final reports sit on desks without review and recommendations are never implemented.
2) *Staff support*. At least one employee should be allotted the time needed to coordinate the group and to organize the data-collection process.

This chapter reviews the purpose of these task forces, their composition, structure, meeting agendas, and outcomes.

Purpose

The ability of a task force to accomplish its goals depends as much on the "force" behind it as on the specific "tasks" assigned to it. The demand from above is probably the strongest force, but the dedication and, perhaps, frustration of the members provide ample fuel. The frustrating part of the ex-

perience was best expressed by an executive who compared working with employees on task forces to a steam locomotive with a big load of cars. A head of steam creates the needed momentum, but then someone refrains from throwing the switch that would keep the momentum going. In other words, all of the effort does not allow management to implement its commitments because of a lack of follow-through.[1]

The following example, drawn from a large, chemical firm's own description, is typical of company task forces and illustrative of how companies approach family issues:

"*What We Do* Our search for excellence lies in working with management to help employees balance the needs of their family and work lives. Our primary focus at this time is child care. In line with our child-care focus, the Pro-Family Benefits Committee set out the following tasks:
(l) Explore the universe of child-care options
(2) Explore Company's, as well as competitive companies' involvement in child care."

"*Who We Are*: The Pro-Family Benefit Committee is one of the satellite committees of the Company Morale Committee, which grew out of the Company's Search for Excellence program. This program is dedicated to providing the type of corporate culture that is responsive to both the needs of its customers and employees, with the end result being a more rewarding and profitable place to work."

In larger corporations, the task force often goes through many incarnations. Members of earlier task forces surmised a number of possible reasons for their failure—the wrong people, no money, "we couldn't find the right solution." Beneath these reasons, they all agreed that the most significant factor preventing success was timing: The company was not yet ready to address family issues at the workplace. The history of task forces at Hewlett Packard and Digital are not uncommon. (See box on page 12.)

---

[1] Rosabeth Moss Kanter, *Changemasters: Innovation for Productivity in the American Corporation*. New York: Simon and Schuster, 1983, p. 120.

Composition

Most companies form task forces composed of the "interested" and the "powerful," as one company manager said. As noted earlier, others, such as ARCO Alaska, include community representatives on their task forces. Still another type of task force is formed by one company that solicits membership from neighboring companies in the community.

A type of task force discussed more briefly in this report is one created by a government agency or community organization in which companies are invited to participate and contribute to solutions that improve family services in the community. The self-interest of the company is served to the degree that employees of the company can take advantage of newly created services. One human-resource manager commented that: "It is sometimes easier to get a corporate contribution to a community program than it is to change benefits when management is leery about involvement in family issues." Since task forces cannot help but educate their members, even communitywide task forces that include company representation may lead to changes in internal corporate policy.

When considering the various kinds of research expertise that might be valuable, the following company functions were found represented on company task forces:

- Human resources (benefits, personnel, employee counseling program, medical, corporate recruiter)
- Community affairs
- Public affairs
- Government affairs
- Training and development
- Corporate research
- Corporate librarian
- Legal counsel
- Corporate treasurer
- Labor relations

The Emerging Task Force

Hewlett Packard Company

- Interest in children and their care and health has always been demonstrated by Hewlett Packard (HP) founders, especially Lucile Packard.
- Under the HP contributions program in the 1960's, several child-care grants were made.
- In late 1977, a division general manager raised the issue of child care with a manager in government affairs. That manager pulled together an internal task force composed of corporate, division and affirmative-action representatives. The task force did not feel it was appropriate for HP to sponsor child care directly, but did feel it appropriate for HP to: (1) provide and publicize information about local child-care programs; and (2) contribute to nonprofit providers through its regular contributions program and encourage other companies and foundations to join the effort. This policy was approved by the Vice President, Personnel, and has remained in effect over the years.
- Awareness, interest level, and media coverage have increased in the public and private sectors.
- Recently, the Vice President, Personnel requested a review of HP's child-care policy and a task force was formed for this purpose:

General Mission Statement

"This task force is broad in scope. We will review and discuss HP's current child-care policy and alternatives. We will make a recommendation on what HP's involvement should be regarding child care to the Vice President and to the Employee Benefit Committee of the HP Board of Directors."

The Reappearing Task Force

Digital Equipment Corporation

"Over the past five years, Digital has come to understand that the child-care issue is a very complex one that requires a very carefully planned response on the part of the company. During this period, a number of task forces were established to sensitize the company to the issues and make recommendations. Currently, many organizations within the company have flexitime in place, part-time and job-sharing situations, work-at-home experiments, and personal leave-of-absence options for employees.

"As we look into the future, it is clear that Digital must become more pro-active in addressing these issues, yet not get in the child-care business (i.e., on-site child-care facilities). We need to establish a clear company policy statement on child care and begin to implement plans and programs across the company in a consistent and equitable manner in support of that policy. We must carefully review our existing personnel policies to ensure they adequately address our employees who have child-care needs.

"Over the next few months, the Child Care Task Force will be discussing these problems throughout the company in an effort to enhance our understanding and sensitivity toward these issues. Also, the task force will make specific recommendations to the Personnel Management Committee concerning what the company's short-term, medium-term, and long-term strategies should be in addressing these issues. These recommendations will include an overall company policy and programs that will support that policy."

Corporate Employee Relation
Program Manager,
Digital Equipment Corporation

The number of people on a company task force will depend on the politics of the organization, as well as on the number and location of employees. The sizes of task forces studied for this report ranged from six to twenty members. In general, the smaller groups were found to be more productive and more efficient. But a larger group that represents a wider variety of functions, levels and expertise within the organization may improve the quality of the output and ensure the successful implementation of recommended programs.

Some companies leave task-force membership fluid, though maintaining a core of responsible staff. The task force on child care at A T & T includes at least one representative from each division of the company. When it became clear that additional staff from various divisions were very interested in the subject, they were allowed to participate on an ad hoc basis. At Hewlett-Packard Company, the task force is made up of a representative from several company sites, one person from government affairs (who was familiar with the subject matter, having served on previous task forces), and others with needed expertise. Other companies closed membership when it was felt that they had achieved adequate representation by sex, racial group, job category, location, and so on.

The membership-selection process depends largely on who is organizing the effort. Assuming that management's support is important, there undoubtedly will be requests for the inclusion of senior management. Task-force initiators may know people in the organization who have expertise in the area, either by virtue of their family relationships or their work responsibilities. Obviously, having parents on the task force is useful for getting feedback on program ideas and clarifying work-family issues.

In a company where task forces are a way of life, there may be a formal selection process. At Norwest Bank in Minneapolis, membership is open to anyone in the bank. Articles published in the weekly newsletter and memos and presentations by managers encourage employees to apply. For the bank's 1983 task force on work and family issues, an estimated 125 applications were submitted (approximately 6 percent of the bank population).

The bank's selection committee comprised eight volunteers, who had served on previous task forces. The view was: "Don't have top management hand pick people, or nobody will trust what the group comes up with." Each applicant was interviewed by a member of the selection committee, who considered both individual and group characteristics. According to one of the managers interviewed: "We make sure the person has something to offer. They don't need to have considerable background in the subject, but they should have given it some thought. They also need the energy and ability to make a commitment."

The second consideration in selection is the composition of the group. As one executive describes the situation: "We want a good balance of men and women and of racial groups. It has been harder finding older, longer-term employees.

Most applicants tend to be the younger, newer folks with a lot of energy. We typically get some conservative views represented from those who want to make sure nothing too radical happens. We also look for the kinds of personalities that will make the group fun."

Structure

Task forces generally appoint a chairman who is responsible for alerting other members of meetings, maintaining focus and momentum, meeting deadlines, and communicating with senior management. This individual might be selected by the task force itself once it is formed. But, in most cases, the chairman was appointed by a senior manager before the task force began its work. In the case of Norwest Bank, the selection committee picked the chairman—with management's approval. "Our thinking was that we needed to have somebody we know who has some leadership ability and who was perceived as credible by top management," a company executive said.

The group generally breaks down into subcommittees in order to maximize its time, expertise and resources. At the beginning, committees tend to be organized by the type of information needed: for example, parent needs, community resources, other company programs. Once the data have been collected, the committee then reorganizes itself to prepare for analysis. Committee structure then reflects possible outcomes, such as benefits, work policies, and community partnerships.

Timing

Since a task force, by definition, generally meets until the task is completed, definition of the task becomes all important. If the task force is charged with coming up with a recommendation for family-supportive solutions, presumably its work is complete when the final report is submitted. Many task forces recommend immediate action on some priority issues and then request additional time and resources to conduct further research and recommend additional programs.

Generally, a task force works for a complete year. But the process could be lengthier than anticipated, particularly when top managment support is lacking, when unforeseen circumstances arise, or when no outside expertise is utilized. It is most important, executives report, to have clearly articulated responsibilities as interest wanes among the members and inertia sets in. Sometimes, for example, due to mergers, layoffs or resignations, membership on the task force changes. These interferences with the continuity of the group may increase the workload and the time commitment required.

Individual task-force members make considerable investments of time in task-force activities. Some task forces were found to meet weekly or bi-monthly, although most were convened once per month. Subcommittees met more regularly and individuals were responsible for additional work on their own.

The deadline for submission of recommendations may be predetermined by the appointing executive. Some may select individuals who cannot afford to spend considerable time on the effort and are thus forced to work efficiently. At ARCO Alaska, Inc. there are yearly goals for the task force, which ends when the task is completed.

Agenda

The first step for most task forces is to educate the members about the nature of the problem and possible solutions. All of the information about how the issue emerged is helpful, along with any data collected during the preliminary research phase. The granules of ideas collected in the early phases will quickly grow into mountains of articles, reports and correspondence. This educational process might also be

Decision-Making in a Labor-Management Committee

A union-management day-care committee at the Bureau of National Affairs (BNA), an employee-owned private publishing company, led to the founding of a child-care information and referral network for the entire Metropolitan Washington, D.C. area. The joint committee grew out of the 1982 contract negotiations between BNA and The Washington-Baltimore Newspaper Guild, which represents all non-management, non-sales employees at the company. It was ageed that the study would take place on company time, and that its expenses would be borne by the company.

With three management appointees and three Guild members, the committee began work in March, 1982, meeting every two weeks until mid-Fall. In addition to meetings, committee members reviewed relevant literature, contacted experts in the field, attended seminars, and visited child-care agencies.

The committee discussed a range of child-care issues and program solutions, including information and referral, subsidies, flexitime, use of sick leave for sick child care, on-site centers, and tax assistance. There were three outcomes of the committee study: (1) An innovative child-care referral service; (2) permission for employees to use their sick leave to care for sick children; and (3) a company effort to adapt working schedules to child-care needs where possible.

The Guild had hoped for more, particularly some sort of child- care subsidy. In the report, it declared: "...Pre-imposed financial constraints limited the flexibility of management representatives to consider seriously which options would best benefit BNA employees... The management representatives apparently had no clearance to talk seriously about proposals involving outlays of money exceeding a few thousand dollars."

Management replied that the committee was not authorized to spend benefit dollars, and that an additional monetary benefit, such as a subsidy, would have to be bargained for in future contract negotiations: "If the company did not agree to a day-care benefit at the bargaining table, it is not logical to expect it to regard itself as obliged to confer one outside negotiations."

Although committee members had worked in a non-adversarial way, positions hardened as it came time to report. Thus, the March, 1983 committee report contained separate union and management positions on nearly every issue discussed.

(1) Information and Referral Outcome

The Metropolitan Washington Council of Governments (COG) agreed to serve as the headquarters for a network of child-care referral agencies for the entire area. BNA contributed $5,000 to get the service started, and hosted a meeting to encourage other employers to contribute. With a total of $20,000 from employers and an appropriation from the public jurisdictions via the COG budget, the Metropolitan Washington Child Care Network began as an innovative private/public partnership.

Management committee members felt that "the information and referral network may bring to light numerous unknown or hitherto-unappreciated facts concerning day care. There appear now to be no reliable data on the day-care needs of the working-parent population, including the BNA workforce."

The union representatives, for their part, commended management for the effort, noted their own pride at having participated, but stated that "the relatively small direct benefit to BNA employees does not fulfill the company's obligation to its employees to provide some child-care assistance."

Management replied that it had no such obligation until a bargained contract said it did.

(2) Sick Child Care Assistance

"Management and the union agree that sick children present serious problems to employed parents," the committee reported.

The union presented a three-part proposal: (a) a subsidy of up to $20 per day for up to five days per year to help parents pay for sitters for their sick children; (b) allowing parents to use their sick leave if they prefer to stay home with their sick children; and (c) assisting parents to find a reliable sitter, either through a listing at BNA or through an arrangement with an outside agency.

It was agreed to recommend that employees be allowed to use up to five days of their sick leave for children's illnesses. The five-day limitation was dropped by management because of the anticipated difficulty in policing it, and the availability of sick days for use in caring for sick children.

There was some discussion in the committee of extending this benefit to illnesses of all dependents, but management representatives felt that was outside the scope of the committee.

Management raised the issue of legal liability in response to the babysitter registry proposal, and expected the new COG Network to provide such a referral list. Union representatives countered that that was an "unrealistic" hope, since "few I & R services around the country perform this function."

(3) Flexitime

The Guild proposed that a policy favoring flexitime should be adopted, and that it should be implemented by hiring a consultant-facilitator to work with supervisors and employees to devise flexitime programs. Management did not agree to the suggested implementation idea, but committee members did agree to recommend this policy statement:

"BNA encourages flexitime scheduling consistent with the needs of the workplace in those units where the nature of the work does not make it unduly awkward or expensive. Supervisors shall make every effort consistent with unit efficiency to accommodate employees' preferences. Special consideration shall be given to parents seeking to adjust their schedules in order to ease the burden of arranging child care."

While approving this recommendation, union representatives expressed concern over its implementation, and urged union officers and members "to work actively with supervisors to achieve appropriate working schedules." Management representatives noted that flexitime already existed in many BNA units, and acknowledged that some managers may need some encouragement and instruction to consider flexitime use.

(4) Subsidies

As a way of increasing the affordability of high quality child care, and a "an attractive alternative to an on-site child-care center," the union proposed that BNA subsidize 40 percent of employees' child-care costs. This, they said, was likely to amount to $30 per week for infants and $24 per week for preschoolers. They estimated the cost would not exceed $100,000 per year.

Management said its rejection of the subsidy proposal was based on, (a) its availability to a limited number of employees; (b) its expense, given relatively high salaries and benefits at BNA; (c) suspicion of possible fraud; and (d) concern about the "political statement" that subsidies make in encouraging greater use of non-parental child care.

(5) On-Site Center

The Guild concluded that a center located at or near the work site would be "a first-class option," although it might be difficult to establish given the costs and the highly residential area around BNA's headquarters. Such a center might attract not only BNA employees but those from other companies, they suggested.

Management representatives had stated at the outset that BNA was unwilling to consider establishing an on-site center, for a variety of reasons: (a) There would have to be two centers, given BNA's two sites; (b) high cost; (c) concern over liability insurance; and (d) potential underutili-

zation. Thus, the issue of a center was quickly dismissed in the committee's deliberations. In preparing its part of the final report, however, the union suggested a new strategy: BNA could put a child-care center in the new building it was planning, and use that fact to gain from the D.C. zoning board an exception to height limitations for the building. Management felt that would be an "anti-community move" with substantial adverse public relations results.

(6) Taxes

The committee considered the effects of the 1981 Economic Recovery Tax Act and possible implementation of a salary reduction plan for child-care expenses. A member of BNA's Tax Management staff, a tax lawyer well versed in the Act, concluded that the salary reduction plan would be advantageous to BNA employees if the Internal Revenue Service published regulations permitting such plans. The committee agreed to wait for such regulations before formally proposing such a plan.

In the period since 1983, BNA has actively supported the Metropolitan Washington Child Care Network, and has contributed also to the local agency providing child-care referrals in the suburban county where its secondary building is located. One management member of the original committee has provided the oversight for these efforts. Union interest has waned between contract bargaining sessions.

In 1984, when bargaining for a new two-year contract, the Guild proposed that BNA provide a child-care subsidy, similar to the one proposed in committee. They also proposed that the contract stipulate the new company policy about use of sick leave for caring for sick children, and that it be broadened to include illnesses of other family members.

The Guild reported that their members had had an overwhelmingly positive response to the use of sick leave for sick children. Management, on the other hand, reported that supervisors had complained about the new policy, and that it should not be extended beyond sick children.

After some debate about the further need for the committee, it was agreed: (a) to continue the committee so it could study child-care issues as they arose; and (b) to include the use of sick leave for children's illnesses in the contract. The subsidy proposals and the proposal to expand sick leave to others illnesses were dropped.

In the 1986 bargaining, the Guild surfaced its proposal about extending sick leave to illnesses of "other members of the household," which was not approved. They also proposed a salary reduction plan for dependent-care expenses, now that the IRS was allowing employers to go ahead with such plans, although final regulations were not yet issued. Management recognized the benefits of salary reduction, but felt that the payroll system could not accommodate it. With a new payroll system in the planning stages, management anticipated being able to look at the possibilities at a later time.

Report of the Joint Committee on Day Care, Washington, D.C.: Bureau of National Affairs, Inc. and Washington-Baltimore Newspaper Guild, Local 35, March 15, 1983.

accomplished by bringing in community experts to discuss various aspects of the problem or various solutions.

The three basic categories of subsequent efforts include:

- analyzing the company
  —competing interests
  —related interests
  —management's attitudes
  —unique features of the organization
- determining parent needs
  —current family arrangements
  —areas of work-family conflict
  —preferences for support services
- assessing existing community resources
  —adequacy of supply
  —affordability
  —accessibility
  —quality

(See Chapter 4 for more on how companies acquire such information.) The agendas for task forces at Hewlett Packard and ARCO Alaska, provide a glimpse of the simplicity or complexity of task-force research activities.

ARCO ALASKA, INC.
Dependent Care Task Force
1987 Goals

- Track legislation being introduced relating to selected dependent care issues at the Municipal, State and Federal levels. Formulate draft legislation and obtain sponsorship in areas in which existing legislation is inadequate.

- Collect and disseminate information on dependent care issues. This includes publishing the Working Families Newsletter, hosting brown bag seminars, instituting and maintaining a dependent care hotline, and facilitating a parents network.

- Determine feasibility and coordinate implementation, if appropriate, of a dependent care assistance program as provided for in Section 129 of the Internal Revenue Code.

- Facilitate the development and effective communication of Arco's philosophy regarding dependent care issues to Arco employees and supervisors.

- Provide information on senior care and related issues.

- Evaluate the effectiveness of Child Care Connection referal services.

- Continue child care advocacy role in the community.

- Determine feasibility and support development, if appropriate, of a sick bay facility in Anchorage. This facility would provide "day care" for children while they are ill.

HEWLETT PACKARD
Task Force Schedule

Date	Time	Comments
12/17		Advanced reading packet mailed
1/8	9:30-2 pm	Informational meeting
1/21	1-4 pm	Discussion of options, consultant from The Conference Board, presents the range of child-care options.
2/5	1/2 day	Determine objectives and philosophy
2/25	1/2 day	Draft recommendations

Communitywide Task Forces

In an effort to involve the private sector in community activities, company representatives are often invited to join leaders from other sectors on a task force. This group usually is responsible for conducting research to determine the feasibility of establishing new programs. There sometimes is the expectation that corporate members of the task force will contribute time as well as money to the initiative.

The conveners of these communitywide task forces include United Way, chambers of commerce, local foundations, government agencies, service organizations, and educational institutions. Companies are selected for participation based on their prominence in the community, previous or current provision of family-support programs, their attendance at local conferences on related subjects, or their responses to surveys.

In 1984, ten downtown employers in Sacramento, California participated in a survey of employee child-care needs conducted by the Child Care Coalition, a local advocacy organization. The findings led to the creation of a Mayor's task force, whose responsibility was to suggest ways to expand services to parents working in the downtown area and to educate public and private employers about the need for quality child-care services. The Mayor was motivated by a concern for city employees, as well as for the economic health of the downtown area.

Community politics can play a large role in the design of these task forces. For this reason, they are often larger than internal company task forces to assure representation from all stakeholders in the community. For example, in 1985, the Mayor's Task Force on Child Care in Austin, Texas, comprised 80 representatives and 16 resource people from the community child-care field and business. The following year, the Austin City Council appointed a 15-member Child Care Commission to oversee the implementation of the task force's recommendations. In New York State, Governor Mario Cuomo convened a Commission on Child Care in 1984 to recommend state policies that would improve the state's child-care delivery system. One of the principal agenda items was to encourage private-sector involvement. I.B.M., Con Edison, Morgan Guaranty, and American Express had representatives serving on this 60-member commission.

Some of these task forces end when the research phase is completed; others continue or reorganize to design and implement needed programs. A joint Business Leadership Task Force and United Way Child Care Committee in the San Francisco Bay Area led to the creation of a Child Care Leadership Group responsible for promoting a more "hospitable environment" for the development and provision of child-care services. They were to accomplish this by assessing and then acting upon issues that affect child-care provision. Towards this end, as of January, 1987, they had established a corporate resource bank and were monitoring regulatory policies that affect employer initiatives.

In several cases, the task force has been convened for the purpose of designing a specific program. These are often called "consortium arrangements." (See page 30.) The United Way Downtown Business Consortium Child Care Task Force of Los Angeles defined the responsibilities of corporate members serving on the task force as follows:

(1) The task force is charged with performing a one-time, six-month intensive community service relating to solving a recognized unmet need. The limited time, therefore, requires the representation of those in charge of human resources within downtown's corporate structures, close enough to the top to reflect management's views quickly and accurately. If successful, the downtown model will be proposed in each metropolitan area served by United Way.

(2) Participation implies no commitment by the member company to the eventual consortium program proposed. Corporate participants should be adequately briefed on the problem and its proposed solution so that they can become spokespeople to the United Way Board and, perhaps, to the public.

(3) The United Way Board has sent a Board member, and not a surrogate executive or volunteer, to lead the task force. It expects an equally high level of representation from the corporations who agree to serve as members.

Chapter 4
Assessing Family Needs

Determining family needs is perhaps the most important and most sensitive component of the research process. The company tries to conduct the inquiry in a manner that will not raise expectations, since there is no guarantee that the company can provide solutions to the needs uncovered. Primary sources of information about employee needs and their strategic use are available from internal and external data sources, employee surveys and focus groups.

Data Sources

Source	Strategy
Government	• Project national demographic data to the employee population from data generated by U.S. Bureau of the Census, Bureau of Labor Statistics, and others.
Company	• Collect information from company divisions where employees might have expressed their family concerns (e.g. counseling programs, insurance claims, exit interviews, etc.)
Employees	• Survey employees • Conduct focus groups
Managers	• Interview or survey managers to determine where family problems affect work behavior.
Community	• Based on gaps in community services, determine where employees are likely to face problems.

Multiple sources of information are needed, managers report, because of the reticence of many employees to express their family concerns openly. Because of their reluctance to come forward with ideas, employers devise strategies that respect the privacy of the employee, but that also provide insight into the range of family issues confronting employees.

Government Sources

The Census Bureau has the most reliable data on the family demographics of the population. Census tapes are available for purchase and manipulation. Data services also provide geographically specific information. Other organizations serving families in the community may already have analyzed Census data for the community in question. State agencies may also have demographic information that can be used to project needs within a particular employee population.

It is useful to review the incidence of:

- *Two-earner families*
- *Single parents*
- *Working mothers*
- *Working fathers*
- *Children whose mother work.* Distinctions are usually needed among those with children under the ages of thirteen, six, and three. The number of children under the age of six is the standard number used to substantiate the need for child-care services. School-age services are typically needed for those with children ages six to twelve. A high number of parents with children under three may indicate the need to focus on parental leaves and infant-care services that may be lacking in the community.
- *Adoption*
- *Elderly.* Those above 65, and particularly those above 85, for whom services are most often lacking. These senior citizens may be cared for by family members who are employed.
- *Handicapped people*

Companies can assess the ability of the current population to afford needed services and make future projections about the demands for services with data on average family income, costs of raising a family in today's economy, and the birth rate.

If a firm's work force has a substantial concentration of women, then certain statistics can be weighted to account for the variance between the national and individual firms' employee populations. Companies that relied on Census data caution that these data include all people who work regardless of the type of employment or the number of hours worked. The profile of employees who are employed full time in the labor force may differ greatly from national Census data.

Internal Data on Family Needs

A variety of sources within the company can provide demographic data or some insight into possible work-family strains. Very few companies have their personnel records organized according to the family structure of employees. But employers already have some knowledge about families through insurance claims, counseling programs, tax records, and child-support payments. While much of this information is confidential and may not be reviewed by unauthorized company personnel, aggregated data offer some indication of the scope of needs.

Internal data, merged with Census data, can provide some general estimates about the number of female employees likely to bear children during their work careers. For instance, if 60 percent of the work force is female, and 80 percent of these women are between the ages of 21 and 40, a general estimate of child bearing can be determined. National data indicate that approximately 75 percent of these women will get pregnant at some time during their employment. For a work force of 1,000 employees, that would mean that among the 600 female employees, approximately 360 would have children while employed at the company—or, that more than one-third of the entire work force might need maternity leave at some point.

Another use for internal data is to highlight the kinds of family problems facing workers. It is possible to identify units in the organization where issues may have emerged but were left unaddressed. For instance, an examination of exit-interview records might indicate that some employees resigned because of family problems. Further investigation may show that many of these employees worked in the same division. An extended study may show that a family problem has been "caused by" or "frustrated by" either a company policy or division attitude.

Other sources of internal data on family needs is found in:

- *Employee counseling programs.* The managers of such programs may be able to shed light on the degree to which some seemingly work-related problems were, in fact, caused by family strain or, conversely, how a family problem was created from work demands.
- *Anonymous hotlines or suggestions boxes.* Some employees feel safer raising family concerns without identifying themselves. The nature of those requests for help can yield interesting data on the type of family problems experienced by employees.
- *Health records and insurance claims.* A review of these records can reveal useful data on the health status of various dependents. Employee confidentiality must be respected, but aggregate data may be enlightening. This process of "turning every stone" in the organization familiarizes researchers with companywide data resources while sensitizing managers to family issues. The process of asking questions about employees' family concerns causes managers to ponder the connection between work and family life and, perhaps, listen

more keenly in the future for any signs of work-family strain.

- *Company recruiters.* The kinds of questions and issues raised by candidates for employment may provide insights into the needs of a future work force. For example, at one firm, recent MBA graduates' inquiries about maternity-leave policy led one company to reevaluate its policy.

The Survey

Most companies find there is no better way to understand the family needs of employees than by asking them directly. Nearly any survey is a conspicuous and obtrusive method of research. For this reason, companies conduct surveys only if they are clearly needed to satisfy an objective, and if the company is serious about responding to employees' identified problems. Company managers caution against using a survey for exploratory research. The informational payoff is too low, they say, and the costs are too high. Before a survey is launched, companies tend to clarify the following issues:

(1) What is the real commitment of the organization to the subject of addressing family concerns at the workplace? Surveys can raise expectations about a corporation's response. The fear of raising expectations—and not being able to follow through—is probably the primary reason companies avoid surveys.

(2) Is a survey the best—or only—way of obtaining needed information? In a large organization, management may be satisfied with projections based on national data. Internal data may be sufficient if reviewed along with responses to questions posed during employee focus groups. Some companies, for example, implement counseling or referral services for the purpose of collecting information from employees over time.

Face-to-face interviewing can yield far richer data than might be generated from surveys. For example, Steelcase Inc. considered building a child-care center, but was advised by consultants that other child-care needs might be more pressing. They established an in-house child-care referral service that helped parents choose appropriate child care. After a year it became clear that most parents preferred family day care homes to centers. The company continued its referral program and began an equipment-loan program to assist family day-care providers. This method, however, only allows users of the service to provide input. A company may also want to solicit the views of employees who do not use the service.

IBM felt that a survey was not necessary. The number of women in their work force was increasing and they recognized that the number of dual career and single-parent families in the nation's work force had grown rapidly and would continue to grow. They assumed that the employee population in a large, multi-sited company like IBM reflected demographic trends in society. A T & T, on the other hand, with

326,000 employees wants information beyond demographic totals. Its survey is designed to elicit detailed information on the sources of work-family conflict and the degree of management support for a company response.

Survey Design

The survey should relate specifically to the information needed for decision making. The following research questions, companies report, are useful guides to the selection of questionnaire items:

I. What is the scope of need?
II. What is the nature of family needs?
III. How do family issues affect the bottom line?
IV. Will there be resistance to company involvement?
V. How should the company respond?

Scope of Need

The questions asked to determine the scope of need pertain to the number of employees who have families or are planning to have them, and to the configuration of their families (for example, single parents, dual earners, caregivers for the elderly) and whether there are differences among divisions, regions, jobs or income categories of employees. Answers to questions should provide a demographic and a work history of the employee population.

Demographic Profile: Basic demographic information includes the sex, age, race, number of dependents, and marital status of the employee. It also may be important to establish whether the employee is "living with a partner" in order to determine whether there is another adult income earner in the household. A special set of questions may be needed for divorced or separated parents whose children live with them on an occasional basis.

It is possible that those who are currently expecting children, or who plan to have children within the next two to five years, might also avail themselves of family-support programs offered by the company. It may be desirable to separate the questions posed to expectant parents from those with current child-care needs. The former group's answers are hypothetical, the latter based on actual experience. One firm's questionnaire that surveyed all employees— nonparents, expecting parents, and current parents—separated the survey for each group by using a different colored paper for each group.

Family income is, obviously, another critical piece of information for determining the need for assistance. However, managers say it is better to ask this question late in the survey—perhaps when questioning employees about the cost of the current child-care arrangements. It is important to distinguish between "gross household income" and the salary of the employee.

Work History and Responsibilities: These questions help to determine how families' needs break down among job categories, divisions or plant locations of the company. They may also help to assess the employees' attachment to the job as indicated by the number of hours worked, the length of the career, and the number of interruptions along the way. Inclusion of commuting time in the hours worked and the method of transportation used may be important for those considering an on-site day-care center. For instance, those relying on public transportation are less likely to commute with their preschoolers in order to use a new worksite center.

Educational achievement is another measure of labor-force attachment. Some research suggests that educational background is also related to the form of child-care selected.

Nature of Employees' Family Needs

One way to get information about what employees need is to ask them about their current arrangements for dependents while they work. This type of analysis, executives say, requires a keen, knowing eye in order to identify the gaps in employees' work-family schedules and arrangements.

Employees often rely on more than one form of care each week or even each day. They may also have more than one dependent, so that it is particularly important to know about the care arrangements for each dependent. It is also important to define terms. Parents may refer to anyone caring for their children as "babysitters," while the child-care field has developed its own set of job titles describing various forms of care. Great care is taken to avoid these semantic hurdles in the questions asked.

Having established current use of service programs, the survey might next investigate various problem areas. The logical sequence is to begin with the search for care and then evaluate the employee's level of satisfaction with what was found.

Questions can probe the method and the difficulty in making care arrangements. They also provide insight into the employee's ability to make use of community resources, as well as the adequacy of those resources. Companies say that these are important questions for evaluating resource and referral services and for identifying gaps in community services. A particularly useful question concerns the length of time it took to find care. This can help explain the process to managers who have never had to search for care.

For any company considering child-care services, it is important, managers state, to establish the level of satisfaction with current child-care arrangements. This will help to indicate whether the parent might be willing to leave a current provider and enroll in a newly developed program. However, parental satisfaction with child care is one of the more difficult items to measure. Few parents want to admit to keeping their children in an unacceptable child-care situation. Such an admission can imply the notion of "neglect." Companies report that when the question is posed ("Are you satisfied with your current child-care arrangements?"), 75 percent or more provide an affirmative response. Instead, if the question is broken into component parts, and asks a series of questions about specific aspects of the care arrangement, the parent usually feels more free to express discontent with a part of the program without impugning the entire situation.

Employees' back-up arrangements are important to their satisfaction with their regular form of care. The likelihood of missing work and being terribly inconvenienced is considerably lessened when employees prepare for the inevitable last minute change in programming.

Geographic convenience is an important factor in child-care selection. For some, a long commute provides opportunities for the parent and child to spend some time together; for others, it is a nightmare. Firms ask questions to assess the levels of stress and convenience associated with day-care transportation.

What employees spend on care can be very valuable in establishing the pricing structure for new programs and estimating the potential use of vouchers, scholarships or flexible benefit plans. Such data help determine the affordability of care for the majority of employees.

The questions described above help to establish the current scheduling, logistics and levels of satisfaction with current care arrangements. Firms then seek to ask employees about the degree to which these responsibilities affect their work.

Family Issues and Productivity

Self-evaluations from employees provide a useful measure of how family issues affect work behavior. These questions assess the potential effects of family responsibilities on absenteeism, turnover, tardiness and stress. Answers to these questions also help identify the specific family or work condition that is the source of conflict. For instance, when asking how often the employee missed work because of child care problems, the company can determine whether the problem was associated with a sick child or the lack of back-up assistance. The company can also learn whether the inflexibility of work hours contributed to advancement limitations for those with family responsibilities.

Employee Views on Company Involvement

Depending on how much actual feedback the company wants on family issues, some firms have attempted to determine employees' and managers' attitudes about company support to employees. Questions along this line have appeared on more recent company surveys.

Some company executives believe that mid-level managers and supervisors should play an active role in decision making on work-family issues. Their reasoning is that supervisors hear about these problems from employees. Further, lack of support from mid-management might interfere with the implementation or utilization of programs. For these reasons, some companies make a special effort to solicit the views of supervisors. It is sometimes necessary to consider a separate survey for supervisors or a separate interview (discussed on pages 27-28).

How the Company Responds

The final set of questions (although they might be placed at the very beginning of the questionnaire) concerns the types of programs that employees feel would be most beneficial. These responses may not provide definitive answers, even to the degree that there is overwhelming support for a particular option. The reason for this is that the firm is, in effect, market testing services that do not yet exist. Employees may be unfamiliar with how the programs work. They sound good on paper but, once more information is provided, they may seem less useful or convenient, and may fail to be used by the very employees who expressed great interest in them.

The last warning is given by experienced companies about predicting utilization for on-site day-care centers. Typically, a large number of employees say they will use such a program when asked on a survey. But only 10 to 15 percent of those who say they will use an on-site center show up when the program begins.

There are a number of reasons for this lack of predictability. First, costs may not have been specified. Many employees assume if the program is company-sponsored, it will be free or, at least, less expensive than their current arrangements. Second, it is not always easy for employees to change their current arrangements. For example, the center might open in January and parents do not want to uproot their children mid-year, or perhaps the parents did not consider the morning commute with their young children. The curriculum that was selected may have been thought inappropriate for the child. The largest group of respondents might have been parents of children under age three but the center does not serve this age group. Again, a large portion of those who thought they could use the center cannot do so. Finally, by the time the center opens, the results from the survey may be obsolete. The children for whom parents were responding are older and no longer in need of the same day-care services.

Aside from forecasting limits, the list of possible company responses can provide guidance and direction to the selection of an option. There are a variety of ways to ask the question and much depends on what it is the company hopes to learn. Firms caution against including questions about policies or programs that the company would not introduce under any circumstances.

Survey Structure

Employers may choose to address all of these research questions in one survey. They may first determine general demographics of the employee population and resurvey only those indicating a particular family need. For instance, Wang Laboratories surveyed all employees to identify women over age 35 who had responsibility for an aging parent. These employees were then resurveyed and, eventually, some were selected for inclusion in a pilot program of adult day care for the elderly.

In another instance, the company knew what program it planned to develop and surveyed employees to test their reactions to it. Jack Brown Companies in Austin, Texas, wanted to start a day-care center for its 700 employees. (In working with local governmental officials, an additional fifty slots were to be reserved for community residents.) The company was responding to an investigation made by a consultant where child care was found to be the primary reason for the firm's high absenteeism. A survey was distributed to see how many employees would use the proposed day-care center.

Other employers have chosen to make certain questions optional, recognizing the sensitivity of some issues. For example, VISA surveyed its employees in August, 1982, about their child-care needs. The final portion of the survey, devoted to productivity impact, was optional and was introduced as follows:

> "Part III. Productivity Information. There is very little available on the following topics, which have policy interest for business as well as government. This information could assist other companies in determining whether an employer-sponsored child-care program is desirable. This information is optional and, if provided, will remain confidential." [The questions that followed asked about whether the employee had ever been absent, late, or unproductive on the job because of child-care problems.]

Following general practice, most surveys are first pre-tested on a small group of employees. Pre-testing provides an opportunity to evaluate individual questions, the adequacy of instructions, the rate of and reasons for refusals, and the length of time it takes to complete the questionnaire. Most of the surveys studied were designed so that they could be completed within 15 to 20 minutes. Survey experts report that the response rate drops significantly for those requiring more than 20 minutes to complete.

A major constraint in questionnaire design is the need to respect the privacy of the respondents. Employees must remain confident that their interests and confidentiality are protected. Some companies explain, in a covering letter, that an honest response is in their best interests since they may ultimately lead to policies or programs that help alleviate family problems.

Survey Sample

The decision to survey all employees, or only a sample, depends primarily on the size of the company. In order to assure that the sample is representative of the entire population, this study found that, as a general rule, companies with more than 3,000 employees sampled 10 percent of the employee population, and those with fewer than 3,000 surveyed the entire population.

If there are particular subgroups of the population that must be included, then a stratified random sample should be constructed.[1] For instance, the Medical Area Services Corporation in Boston is the administrative agency for five large hospitals in that city. The corporation was interested in comparing the views of doctors, nurses, administrative staff, and custodial staff. The random samples were selected separately for each of these populations. Another firm was concerned about getting equal representation from various branch offices. Therefore, the employee population was first grouped by region and then randomly selected for inclusion in the sample.

[1] Solomon Dutka, *Notes on Statistical Sampling for Surveys.* New York: Audits and Surveys, 1982.

The Outcome of a Survey: The Transamerica Story

In the early 1980's there were rumblings about child care from Transamerica Life Companies employees, but it wasn't until 1982, when the Los Angeles United Way approached the company about participating in a child-care survey, that interest turned to action. United Way was interested in surveying the child-care needs of employees in the downtown area, and approached downtown employers with a prepared survey instrument. Transamerica was interested, but wanted to learn more than the United Way survey would tell them about their employees' needs. As a result, the company developed a Child Care Task Force to modify the survey to suit company needs.

The survey was distributed in 1983 to all Transamerica employees, 54 percent of whom responded. The second vice president of corporate communications stressed the importance of the cover letter when distributing the survey: "We were very concerned about how the survey would be perceived. If we didn't explain our intentions carefully, some employees might jump to the conclusion that we would open an on-site day-care center the following month.

Our cover letter was worded to assure employees of our interest in helping them, and stressed that no specific solutions had yet been determined."

The task force was responsible for analyzing survey results and applying them to policy and program recommendations. The eight-member task force, representing diverse levels and functions of the company (human resources, law, executive offices, product areas), met from January to March, 1984 until recommendations were developed. The task force submitted its recommendations to the CEO, who approved those initiatives that could be implemented immediately. Other items required further research and a staff person was assigned to oversee their development.

The four primary needs that emerged from the survey were: (1) care for sick children; (2) financial assistance for child care; (3) information and counseling about child-care services; and (4) availability of child-care services. The task force recommended that the company undertake the following:

• Modification of leave policies to allow inclusion of family illness, particularly that of sick children. The

There also might be concern about obtaining a sufficient reponse from women in their child-bearing years, or from other groups that exist in small numbers. For example, professional women in their child-bearing years had previously expressed considerable interest in child care at Procter & Gamble, so the survey sample was weighted to include a higher number of these women. The consultant to Procter & Gamble on this survey, Fran Rodgers, explains the procedure she used in sampling:

> "Employees at each of five sites were grouped into the four following categories: (1) exempt males; (2) exempt females; (3) nonexempt males and (4) nonexempt females. We know in advance that these groups are likely to have dissimilar profiles. All groups had a 10-percent probability of being selected for the sample, except exempt females. This group had a 50- percent probability of being selected, so that we had an adequate number of respondents when analyzed as a separate group. Exempt females were sampled differently due to their relatively small number in the employee population and the special interest they evoke in terms of child-care services. However, when descriptions of the whole company were made, statistical findings for exempt women were weighted back to reflect their true proportions of the whole."[2]

One of the advantages of surveying all employees, or sampling all employee groups, is that it compares the views of parents and nonparents concerning work behavior and attitudes about company support, and gets a picture of the en-

tire population's family configurations. A companywide survey can also help identify a particular employee group to be targeted for special services.

A second consideration in surveying all employee groups is to include those whose families are likely to change in the near future. For instance, some companies devote special sections of their surveys to those who plan to have children, or whose widowed parents are going to come live with them. These are important groups since they will be the ones most likely to use new services. A small bank in the Boston area, concerned about teller turnover, considered child-care provision as a way to recruit mothers of young children. Management believed that these women would provide a stable work force. In order to reach potential employees, the accompanying ad was placed in the local newspaper.

---

[2] Interview with Fran Sussner Rodgers, President, Work/Family Directions and Principal, Rodgers and Associates, Boston, October, 1985.

> ## WOULD YOU WORK
> ## IF YOU HAD CHILD CARE?
>
> Local business is investigating ways to provide child day care services for its employees as a fringe benefit. We would like to hear from you about your child care needs.
>
> If you would be interested in having your child care needs met while you worked in a customer service oriented position, please send your name and address to:
>
> (You will be contacted for further information.)

---

amount of leave should be extended from 15.5 hours to 25 hours. (Implemented immediately.)
- Create a resource and referral (R&R) program by contracting with local R&R agencies. (Implemented immediately.)
- Create a parent-assistance program with a counselor hired on a contract basis for information about parenting. (Implemented immediately as part of existing employee-assistance program.)
- Participate in the planning of a downtown consortium of companies to establish a nearby child-care center. (Still participating as of January, 1987.)
- Include dependent care in a flexible benefits program. (Flexible benefits are under study.)
- Implement a child-care voucher program to reimburse employees for a portion of their child-care expenses. (Under study.)
- Create a child-care center for mildly ill children. Opened on April 7, 1986, Super Care for Kids, as it is called, is a 15-bed infirmary housed within the California Medical Center. The space was bought by Transamerica for one year on a pilot basis. The company pays most of the costs, although employees are charged $10 for the first day of care and $5 for subsequent days for that child or for additional family members.

Both employees and management have been pleased with the company's response. Demand for the referral service has exceeded expectations. The popularity of the parent-assistance program necessitated its expansion by a counselor/nurse practitioner with a background in early childhood development. Although Super Care was favorably received and well publicized, it was initially underutilized. Transamerica now allows employees from other companies to enroll their children in Super Care.

The executive responsible feels that the ongoing success of Transamerica's child- care initiatives should be attributed in part to the survey. She often refers back to data from the survey in order to justify the costs of various programs. She commented: "Without a survey, you run the risk of management pulling the plug on the program. It is essential for substantiating child care as an appropriate company investment with long-term impact."

New Response to an Old Problem: Travelers' Survey on Eldercare

The Travelers Companies has a long history of concern for the aging. In 1979, Travelers hired a firm to examine national trends and recommend one issue upon which the company could focus its resources and business leadership. Aging emerged as the most appropriate issue and the CEO concurred. As a result, The Travelers established its Older American Program and began focusing its energies on the issues of economic security and cost-effective health care for older people.

Aging was consistent with the company's business interests in issues of employment and health. It was an area where the company could make a contribution—and a difference. Support for the aging yielded internal benefits for the company and external benefits for society. A part of the aging issue that became a primary concern was the care-giving responsibilities of Travelers' employees for their aging relatives and friends.

Staff of the Older Americans Program developed a proposal, to be approved by Personnel, for a survey of employees' care-giving responsibilities. The need for such a survey was based on the importance of learning: (1) the extent of care-giving responsibilities among employees; (2) the amount of stress that such responsibilities caused;

and (3) the ways, if any, the corporation could assist employees caring for older people.

Management felt that the survey itself had the potential of enhancing morale: It was good for employees to know that the company cared. There were some concerns about raising expectations regarding a company response, and about the reactions from employees who did not have aging relatives for whom they were responsible. These concerns were unfounded: Employees already knew of the company's commitment to aging issues and were grateful for its investigation of the subject in relation to employees' needs.

Survey results led to the development of several programs to support employee-care-givers:

* A care-giver fair was held where local program providers came to the workplace to inform employees about their services. The fair was attended by 700 employees and retirees. One employee commented: "I got more information in twenty minutes than it would have taken me three weeks to learn." A manager added: "Those hours spent researching available serv-

---

Among 35 responses, 20 mothers indicated a keen interest in working if child care were available. Their responses helped the company to understand the limits of their work hours and other needs. The bank also identified 15 consultants who wanted to help set up the bank's child-care program.

Method of Distribution

The manner in which a survey is distributed to employees will affect the response rate significantly, companies report. The considerations include the cover letter, the appearance of the survey, the method for responding, and the actual distribution of the survey instrument.

The Cover Letter

The letterhead and signature of the cover letter are noticed first. Typically, the company's letterhead is used, but sometimes the consultants hired to conduct the survey will prepare a letter on their own stationery. In such cases, these companies want to assure employees that no one in the company will see the individual responses. One company commented that, while it had considered such a procedure, it believed that it was more important to let employees know that the company had a serious interest in pursuing family-support initiatives—and, it used the company's letterhead.

Most of the cover letters reviewed for this study include a disclaimer of sorts, for example: "The company is merely investigating the need for family assistance and this research

in no way guarantees that the company will be able to respond to identified needs." (See box.)

Distribution

Some distribution strategies generally yield higher response rates, but there are many factors that affect employees' willingness to complete the survey. One of the primary factors is size of the employee population. In a Boston bank, with approximately 120 employees in five branches, the consultants delivered every survey form by hand. In this way they were able to answer any preliminary questions that the employees might have had about the purpose of the survey, and to assure them that an outside group was responsible for analyzing the results. The bank achieved a 90 percent response rate.

A more common practice involves sending the survey through interoffice mail or to the employees' homes. Response rates tend to be higher when they are distributed at the office. If such distribution is made, the company approves of the time off needed to complete the survey. When surveys are sent home, they often get lost or are forgotten, resulting in a lower response rate.

Anonymity

Given the sensitivity of the questions posed, most surveys are filled out anonymously. If names are required, response rates may drop dramatically—and the honesty of answers may also decrease.

ices would probably have occurred during work hours."

- Video-tape kiosks placed around the headquarters provide information on a range of care-giving issues. The interactive video-tape programs have been produced and additional programs will be developed over time.
- Lunchtime seminars on care-giver issues are conducted by staff of the employee assistance program. Four seminars were held in the Fall of 1986.
- A lunchtime care-giving support group is facilitated by employee assistance staff. The company expects that another group will develop in the coming months.
- Travelers' national newspaper for employees and retirees will include a series of articles on eldercare issues.
- A special section on eldercare readings will be added to the corporate library.

Other benefits of assistance to employees caring for older relatives include flexible hours and four weeks of unpaid personal leave. A flexible spending account allows employees to transfer pre-tax dollars from their paychecks into a special account to be used for dependent care expenses.

The company has concentrated its efforts on providing information to employees. There are no intentions to offer direct financial assistance to employees to help them cover eldercare costs, although Travelers' Foundation has supported a variety of aging interests over the years. Funds have been provided to the Connecticut Association of Adult Day Care; The Travelers Center on Aging at the University of Connecticut Health Center, and the National Council on Aging to establish a fellowship program to interest undergraduate medical students in geriatrics and gerontology.

Management's willingness to conduct the survey on eldercare and respond to identified needs was due to two preconditions: The company's history of commitment to older Americans and its provision of child-care information and referral services since 1982. Although management was open to exploring the issue and using a survey to learn more about employees' needs, there was reluctance to ask direct questions about the productivity effects of eldercare responsibilities. As the company representative explains: "It was tempting to ask questions to quantify the time lost at work or the days absent from work because of care giving. However, we felt it was inappropriate for an employer to ask an employee those questions. Employees might have been less willing to complete the survey." The response rate without those questions was 52 percent.

While anonymity is critical, this feature makes it more difficult to target a second mailing, or to request the assistance of those who would like to participate on a task force. A company can overcome the problem of a second mailing by sending a postcard to all employees reminding them of the need to return the survey. Some companies put reminders in the house organ or on bulletin boards.

Other ways to encourage responses are to: (1) ask them voluntarily to print their names somewhere on the survey; or (2) include a tear-off sheet that is to be returned under separate cover.

Response Rate

While most direct-mail surveys have a low response rate, targeted surveys to a specific employee population can yield much higher response rates. This study found companies with response rates that range from a high of 95 percent to a low of 35 percent. Most companies were able to obtain response rates of over 50 percent.

The rate of response depends on many factors. Much depends on whether the survey was mailed or whether employees were required to complete it at the office—the higher response rate occurring with the latter strategy. Perhaps the most important thing recommended by companies is the sincerity with which the companies appear to be interested in addressing employee needs. If this is the fourth survey on the same subject, or if it looks sloppy and there is no effort made to make response easy, then employees will not take the survey seriously.

Focus Groups

The focus group is a useful planning tool, managers say, for bringing together small groups of employees to discuss work and family issues. The primary purpose of focus groups is to add texture to the statistical reports of family needs. The interactive nature of the group helps to amplify patterns identified in employee surveys. It is possible to develop details or insights into ambiguous answers.

American Can first learned about dependent-care issues while conducting focus groups on the firm's cafeteria benefits plan. Focus groups have also been used to supplement general employee attitude surveys. Unisys Corporation (formerly Sperry Corporation) had a series of focus groups called "Roundtable 80's" that helped it to gauge employee perspective on a range of issues facing the corporation in the coming decade.[3]

The focus-group setting also captures the emotional impact and intensity of work-family strains. Most companies believe that these anecdotal reports are invaluable in substantiating the importance of the problem or in justifying a specific recommendation. In the absence of empirical research on the productivity effects of family problems and programs, these group discussions provide important information to strengthen the rationale for such programs.

[3] Barbara Adolf and Karol Rose, *The Employers Guide to Child Care: Developing Programs for Working Parents*. New York: Praeger, 1985, pp. 82-101.

Focus groups also help management to communicate its desires about an appropriate corporate response, and to discover areas where misperceptions exist. Employees often misconstrue the intent of a company policy: Such misunderstandings can be aired in a focus group and communicated to management so they can be corrected.

In 1982, the National Employer Supported Child Care Project identified 24 companies out of 147 with child-care programs that had relied on some form of small-group discussion to measure needs or test reactions to programs under consideration.[4] The managers interviewed report that focus groups may become more widely used because they do not raise employee expectations to the degree that surveys sometimes do.

Structure

Focus groups typically consist of eight to ten people meeting in a two-hour session. Most companies organize groups that include 5 to 10 percent of the employee population. A smaller sample is acceptable when accompanied by a companywide survey. Most companies use "pure groups"—that is, those that separate men and women; hourly and salaried workers; parents and nonparents; and supervisors and subordinates. The "comfort zone" is critical in these discussions and no one should feel inhibited by the presence of other participants. The needs and concerns of these groups may also differ. In one company, the professional staff emphasized problems related to travel and overload. For support staff, the major concerns focused on personal days and eldercare.

Employees from targeted groups may be randomly selected to attend focus groups. Participation is not required—although monetary inducements are occasionally offered to encourage greater attendance. (Fees range from $15-$25 per session.) Sessions are usually held during work hours for maximum convenience. The company typically schedules a series of focus groups over a short period of time. This helps minimize the degree to which responses among groups will differ due to other changes in the organization.

Nearly all companies felt that an outside facilitator should be hired to design, conduct and analyze focus-group sessions. The facilitator works closely with the company managers responsible for the inititative so that analyses of employee discussions reflect the major concerns of the organization. Reports define the major problems raised by employees, provide sample anecdotes, and capture the mood and tone of each group.

A large, nonprofit employer in New York City relied primarily on focus groups to develop a set of recommendations to management regarding new family-supportive initiatives. A memo was sent to senior managers asking if their staffs would be interested in cooperating in some internal

research. A positive response led to the decision to hold focus groups and to encourage people to sign up for them. Six focus groups were organized, three of which were attended by professional staff and the other three by support staff. Approximately 75 people attended the six luncheon meetings.

At least one of the three organizing managers sat in on each session. An outside consultant was hired to run the focus groups and write a report based on the responses. A manager stressed the importance of the outside facilitator: "There is little trust of the personnel division in this organization. The session would have been doomed had personnel conducted them alone. However, this really depends on the organization."

Content

The topics covered depend largely on the purpose of the focus group and its role in the overall research process. If the focus group is a component of a needs assessment, questions will concentrate on current support systems and areas of conflict between work and family responsibilities. If conducted after an employee survey, the discussion may seek to explain survey responses. The questions might also elicit feedback on company policies and programs under review.

Some companies avoid focus groups for fear they will lead to "group gripe sessions." Companies try to avoid this by defining the parameters of the discussion. Comments on unrelated topics, such as pay scales and office accommodations, are often diverted. Sample questions for an inquiry into child care needs might include:

Family and Community Support
- What child-care arrangements do you currently use? What do you like or dislike about these arrangements? What would you recommend to improve them?
- Ideally, what kind of child-care arrangement would you feel most comfortable leaving your child in?
- What kind of support do you get from you spouse or partner, older children, other relatives?
- What happens when an emergency arises, such as when the child gets sick or you face necessary overtime or travel?

Company Support
- How supportive is your supervisor of your family's needs?
- Have there been instances when work was interrupted for family reasons?
- What are the greatest sources of conflict between your work and your family life?
- What would make it easier to balance work and family life?

Limitations of Focus Groups

The primary limitation of a focus group is that it is not "scientific" and cannot give a company a picture of the population as a whole. Some companies interviewed were initially concerned that the information gathered in focus groups

---

[4] Sandra L. Burud, Pamela R. Aschbacher, and Jacqueline McCroskey, *Employer-Supported Child Care: Investing in Human Resources*. Boston: Auburn House, 1984, pp. 77-98; 303-305.

is subject to bias because employees try to respond with the "socially correct" response. After the focus group, most of these companies were impressed with the candor and insight displayed by their employees.

Most managers concurred that the focus group has proved to be a valuable tool in assessing employees' family-support needs. One manager commented: "Our focus groups generated a lot of excitement. Management realized that it was thinking too narrowly—that work and family issues are much broader than we anticipated."

The View From the Middle

The key actors in the decision-making process usually represent the top and bottom of the organization. Employees may raise the issue and then focus on obtaining top management support. Or a senior manager may develop an interest in family issues and seek employee involvement. In most instances, mid-level managers—that is, those with supervisory responsibilities, or with management and no policymaking responsibilities—are initially absent from the process. Many of the companies studied recognize this oversight and strongly recommend that mid-level managers and supervisors be involved at all stages of the decision-making process.

In a 1985 press conference on parental leave policies, sponsored by Catalyst and Touche Ross, Amory Houghton, Chairman of the Executive Committee and retired chairman of Corning Glass Works explained: "I'm worried about the middle level of company operations, not policy announced from the top. How will a line or product manager—with a budget, a schedule, and a quota— respond to a valued employee who announces she's pregnant? The manager depends on her to meet bottom-line pressures, which are tremendous."

This concern emerged in research on early—unsuccessful— efforts to implement flexitime. Middle managers apparently feared the loss of control over punctuality as a measure of job performance. They were unaware of the overall impact that scheduling problems had on the organization and were never acquainted with the intended purpose of flexitime as a solution. This ignorance led to their resistance.[5]

A lack of cooperation among mid-level managers reduced the effectiveness of a parent-involvement program initiated by the Houston School District. The School District wrote to local employers requesting release time so that parents could participate in a tutoring program. The companies complied with the request, but few parents showed up for the school's program. Supervisors assumed that meeting a production quota took priority over time off for parenting. In this case, the supervisors were not involved in the decision making nor were they told about the priorities of the company. As one manager observed: "If they don't accept the problem as legitimate, they won't accept the company's solution to it."[6]

Mid-level managers may never make the connection between certain employee behavior and family problems. But the more astute among them are in a position to shed light on these problems and to help senior management identify the source of work-family conflict and the way in which current policies might be creating new tensions.

Strategies for Involvement

Mid-level managers can contribute to the decision-making process by offering suggestions for new policies and programs that would help employees work more productively. Since employees rarely voice family concerns, it is the supervisory level that may be the most valuable during the decision-

---

[6] See Dana Friedman, *Encouraging Employer Initiatives for Working Parents.* New York: Carnegie Corporation of New York, 1983.

> ### What Managers Really Think[1]
>
> In the Spring of 1984, Bank Street College of Education interviewed a selected number of managers from the Research Division at Merck & Company in Rahway, New Jersey. These interviews were part of a larger study at Merck called *The Corporate Work and Family Life Study.* (See box on page 40.) Managers were asked how they view the increase in the number of working mothers; what they think is the role of corporations in making the changes that will help working-parent families under stress; and what the barriers to corporate change are. The responses indicated:
>
> - Managers are generally not aware of employees' everyday work-family problems: They are more likely to know about severe problems such as divorce or family illness.
> - Many managers are more likely to know about the specific problems of male employees. When explored further, it was found that they may be more likely to respond positively to a man's problem than to a woman's. As one female manager explained: "A lot of managers feel in the back of their minds that, when they hire a woman, she is going to have problems. Managers are expecting problems, which they see as probably initiated by some action on her part. But if a man's having problems, then they are probably genuine."
> - Most managers think that a company must walk a fine line in response to work-family problems—the line between being paternalistic (or interfering) and being responsive. Managers concurred that the company should step in whenever an employee's productivity or performance was affected by personal problems.
> - Most managers feel that the solution to work-family problems lies in the hands of the managers who should have the flexibility to decide what to do.
>
> [1] Source: Ellen Galinsky, Diane Hughes and Marybeth Shinn, *The Corporate Work and Family Life Study.* New York: Bank Street College of Education, 1986, (Executive Summary).

---

[5] Stanley D. Nollen, *New Work Schedules in Practice: Managing Time in a Changing Society.* New York: Van Nostrand Reinhold, 1982, p. 80.

Fact Finding—Some Suggestions

In the course of the present research, it was possible to review 20 questionnaires that had been developed by task forces to implement their fact finding. Human-resource executives report that most consultants seem better versed in their subject matter than they are in designing such instruments. If the consultants are specialists in child care, this is not surprising. Both survey design and sampling have become highly developed specialties in their own right. It seems more likely that the task forces would consult child-care specialists than expert pollsters. In that event, there are some suggestions that should guide questionnaire construction.

(1) The words should be simple, direct and familiar to all respondents. For example, some people do not know their marital status, but they certainly know if they are married, single, divorced, separated or widowed.

(2) Wherever possible, "laundry lists" of multiple choices should be provided. For one thing, this makes analysis easier. For another, some people feel that "writing it down" might help to identify them; others are uncomfortable with the idea of expressing themselves in writing.

(3) Instructions should be simple and clear.

(4) Only one subject should be covered in one question.

(5) If rating scales are used, the "best" answers should not always be in the same place (i.e., at the right margin).

(6) If the questions are not applicable to all respondents, the instructions should be clear as to which groups they are intended for.

(7) Keep the task as short as possible without sacrificing information that may be needed. It is easier to discard a question than to go back to get more information.

One source of material for the questionnaire, including the laundry lists, is the preliminary discussion that the task-force members will have among themselves or with other employees. Notes should be made of specific situations that can be included in the final report as "human interest."

I. Scope of the Need

Characteristics of Employee's Household - Questions can include:
- Employee's marital status
- Employment status of household members and hours worked
- Ages of household members
- Number of children present; related children not present
- Household income
- Plans for (additional) children

Work History and Job Responsibilities
- Department and job title
- Occupational category
- Current annual wage/salary
- Job tenure (current position)
- Hours of work
- Commuting time and arrangements
- Previous positions with company
- Work interruptions during career
- Educational attainment

II. Child Care Needs (Information to be obtained for each child)
- Type of care used
- How current arrangement was located
- Problems encountered in arranging child care
- Child-care services not available (difficult to locate)
- Time spent in locating child-care arrangement
- Back-up arrangements
- Location of child care (proximity to work or home)
- Cost of child care
- Degree of satisfaction with child-care arrangements

III. Effects of Family Issues on Employee's Productivity
- Frequency of absences, tardiness, unproductive time on job due to (specified) child-care problems
- Perceptions concerning amount of work-family stress
- Impact of family considerations on availability for work and career advancement
- Impact of work schedules on work-family stress
- Interest in part-time work
- Degree of support from supervisor in accommodating worker's family needs

IV. Employee Views Concerning the Employer's Role
- In providing child-care assistance
- In developing policies that assist working families
- In expecting supervisors to be responsive to employees

V. Employee Preferences Concerning Employer Responses
- Checklist of range of options and degree of personal interest in them if provided by the company
- Checklist of policies/benefits/services that companies should provide

making process. Besides the use of surveys and focus groups, companies also recommend that a series of individual interviews be held with key managers.

Interviews. A group of senior managers should select "opinion makers" among the management group—people who represent their management group in other settings or who are outspoken about their employees' needs.

Staff from the human-resource division or members of the task force might conduct the interviews. The interview questions pertain to four areas of information: (1) the supervisory responsibilities of the manager; (2) observed areas of work-family conflict; (3) attitudes toward a company response to family-related problems; and (4) recommendations for company policies that would make a difference. The analysis of responses should focus on the degree to which managers are supportive of their employees when family issues arise. The interviews should also measure anticipated cooperation, should the company change policies or implement new programs that require mid-level management support.

Survey. In order to involve mid-level managers in surveys, a draft of the employee survey could be circulated among managers with requests for comments. A separate survey can also be distributed to the management group.

Chapter 5
Identifying Community Resources

The company response to family needs often builds on the community's supply of local services. This may require the creation of new services where none exists, or the augmentation of existing services to correct inadequacies. With the establishment of new services, the company must also decide whether they should be run by the company or by a community agency. An examination of community resources helps identify what gaps exist and which the company can consider filling.

The extent of research required for this component of the decision-making process depends on the scope of the company's intentions—that is, whether it wishes to serve only employees of the company or community residents as well. In the latter case, consumer needs and public policies must also be analyzed if all working families in the community are to have access to the services created by the company.

Some of the companies surveyed warned against the unnecessary duplication of services already available in the community. There have been reports of community groups resenting a company's involvement in child care because new facilities might compete with existing facilities. As one executive asked: "If there is a terrific day-care center up the block that just lost its funding, why should the company build a new center and let the one with 10 years' experience go out of business?"

IBM was aware of shortages of care in many communities when it designed its nationwide child-care referral service. IBM was concerned that its employees might use up many of the available day-care slots in communities where child care was in short supply. Therefore, the program was designed to help stimulate the supply of new services for both IBM employees and other members of the community. But only an investigation into the availability of existing community programs can provide a company with that kind of information.

A look at community resources may also corroborate concerns voiced by employees. For instance, suppose a need for infant care was mentioned repeatedly on surveys and in focus groups. Considered by itself, this finding might cause a company to consider various ways to create new infant-care services. However, a look at the community may reveal several day-care centers and family day-care homes with openings for infants. This information portrays the problem more accurately as one of accessibility and not availability. A resource and referral program would be a more useful response than the establishment of a new infant-care center.

In order to obtain a sense of where employees' children are cared for, employees may be asked to provide the names of their children's care givers. Then a company representative, accompanied by a knowledgeable consultant, can visit such facilities. (The process must be replicated in each community where the company employs workers and intends to offer such services.) Visits to local programs help to define the standard of quality and prevailing fees and wages for programs in that community. This information can verify data provided by employees and also helps to develop standards by which the company might establish its own programs. Most companies interested in developing programs want them to be of high quality. They need to know the competition before a superior product can be produced.

Contact with the community can also help to identify consultants. Knowing the reputations of local providers, and the structure of the delivery system, can help align the company with the best talent and most efficient strategies for implementing the firm's response to family needs.

Community experts also become a link to information about other corporate or public initiatives. Similar initiatives may be being planned by the mayor, the county commissioner, United Way, a local university or college, or other corporations. There may be opportunities to collaborate with these groups and share program costs, risks and benefits.

Finally, a review of local or state policies is recommended by many firms as a useful way of predicting forthcoming change. For example, a 1986 ordinance in San Francisco requires that any new downtown building have a child-care center, or that $1 per square foot be paid by the developer into a child-care fund administered by the city. Having advance information on these kinds of ordinances can save a company time and program expense.

Interviews with local experts can generate information about several types of concerns. Typical of the issues covered are:

- Gaps in community services
- Capacity of local programs—are there waiting lists?
- Cost of local services—are fees affordable to employees, given the level of company salaries and other factors related to the standard of living in that community?
- Quality and status of programs—is there pending litigation, or noncompliance with licensing standards?
- Knowledge of national sources of information

When working with community groups, companies are sometimes concerned about raising expectations prematurely or revealing the current direction of company deliberations. In one instance, the company discussed the possibility of establishing a new, on-site, day-care center with local service providers. The next day, to the company's dismay, the local newspaper announced the company's plans to create a new day-care center. Management was so put off that it cancelled efforts to develop company solutions to child-care needs.

Sources of Community Information

Much of the information about community resources may already be available. The first place to look to (which many companies recommend, but neglect to do themselves) is their own corporate foundations, offices of community affairs, and government-relations units. Human-resource executives may not be aware that the family problem under investigation may have already surfaced in another area of the company, and that prior research may already exist in-house.

Examples of outside information sources about community services include:

- Prominent providers of service, particularly ones used by a number of company employees
- Resource and referral agencies (sometimes known as Community Coordinated Child Care agencies or 4C's in the child-care field, or Area Agencies on Aging for eldercare)
- United Way
- Chamber of Commerce
- Mayor's office
- City council, county commissioner, other government seats with influence over decisions made about social services
- Colleges or universities with relevant departments (e.g. child development, gerontology, social work)
- Business schools
- Professional associations for pertinent fields
- Junior League
- American Association of University Women
- YWCA

- Church groups
- Local personnel associations
- Local grantmaker associations
- Community foundations
- Public school system
- Ancillary services such as hospitals, libraries, counseling clinics, and so on.

Collaboration

When organizations collaborate to produce a family-supportive service, a new dimension of decision making is needed. Groups collaborate out of a desire to share the risks and costs of developing new programs. In doing so they must negotiate a confluence of goals, responsibilities and outcomes. While collaborative programs are more difficult to implement, most agree that the advantages outweigh the disadvantages.

When companies collaborate with other companies, it is often referred to as a "consortium arrangement." An increasing number of companies collaborate with nonprofit and government agencies that look to the private sector to replace what government seems less willing or able to fund. Out of these efforts emerge new community-based services that are available to all families in the community.

The rationales for collaboration, as described by company executives, are listed below:

- *Return on investment*—By making the community a better place to live, employers are able to attract good people and the community benefits from an improved quality of life[1]
- *Credibility*—Collaboration can legitimize and sanction corporate involvement in family issues.
- *Spread the risk*—Collaboration leads to group "ownership" and safety in numbers.
- *Breadth of input*—There is greater likelihood for success where more people contribute to the definition of the problem and its solution. The pool of talent is increased, which is particularly important when the initiators lack certain expertise. The solutions are likely to have broader appeal because of the varied input.
- *Professional growth*—Work with talented peers can be a learning experience, one that engenders a long-term collegial relationship. As one executive said: "Collaboration provides an opportunity to teach and learn at the same time."

Consortium arrangements are attractive to large companies when the primary beneficiary is the community:

- Richardson-Vicks Inc., Emery Worldwide, Perkin Elmer, Home Equity and T-Bar were the five companies that contributed a total of $50,000 to the startup of a com-

[1] See Leonard Lund, *Locating Corporate R & D Facilities*. The Conference Board, Report No. 892, 1986, p. 9.

munity child-care center in Wilton, Connecticut. The state awarded a grant of $20,000, and the town appropriated $50,000 to bring the former school building up to code. Each company received a certain number of slots for its employees, based on the size of the initial contribution.

- The California Child Care Initiative Program, spearheaded by BankAmerica, is an effort to increase the supply of child care throughout the state of California. The program was piloted for one year in five counties at a cost of $700,000 raised from public and private sources. The initiative proved so successful in generating new child-care providers and spaces for children that the program is being expanded to include ten counties starting in 1987. To date, 24 participants—14 companies and 9 public-sector employers—have contributed over $1.5 million to the program. The initiative does not offer

any special considerations or enrollment priorities for participant companies' employees.

Cost sharing may be even more important to smaller companies that are unable to support an initiative on their own. One of the risks that small companies often face is underutilization of a program. Through collaboration, small companies are able to pool their employee populations and thus assure an adequate number of users for the program. This may help explain why a growing number of child-care centers are being developed on a consortium basis within office parks. The park developer may provide some initial funding and the staff to organize the effort. Tenant companies are then requested to support the program on an ongoing basis, or to provide the rest of the needed startup capital. The general partner of the Prospect Hill Executive Office Park in Waltham, Massachusetts, explained his reasons for

---

A Consortium That Never Developed a Program

In 1982, The Austin (Texas) Child Guidance and Evaluation Center received a discretionary grant of $107,416 from the U.S. Department of Health and Human Services to organize six major hospitals in the area into a consortium child-care arrangement. Four of the hospitals agreed to participate. They worked for a year developing a plan of action, but the center never opened. A portion of the federal dollars was returned, and the Austin Child Guidance and Evaluation Center published a report designed to help others avoid some of the pitfalls they had experienced.[1] The lessons learned fall into four categories: cooperation, economic utility, power and conflict.

Cooperation

(1) After a proposal for a child-care consortium has been initiated, "stew time" is useful for allowing members to consider the ramifications of their commitment.

(2) Project planners are responsible for the structure and productivity of this time period, which generally consists of educating members about the benefits, costs and risks of child-care provision.

(3) Early in the process, the group should identify conflicting goals, and work out shared goals.

(4) The degree of ownership must be clear, since it is a reflection of commitment and expectation.

(5) Cooperation within the consortium is influenced by the shared history of the participants: A history of competition can adversely affect the ability of participants to work together.

Economic Utility

(1) Each company must determine whether funds will be contributed as part of the employee benefits package or as a charitable contribution.

(2) The tax and equity considerations must be considered.

(3) Potential members must determine if the noneconomic benefits are worth the actual costs of consortium participation.

Power

(l) Power can be defined as the capacity to limit the choices of others, and can be measured by the resources accessible to the organization.

(2) A consortium has a greater chance for success if the participants have similar levels of power and access to resources.

(3) Powerful consortium members have a "fail safe" mechanism in the knowledge that they have the resources to pursue the initiative alone even if the group effort fails.

(4) A common and effective method of insuring commitment to a project is to require organizations to contribute funds in order to participate.

(5) Representatives must be able to speak and make decisions for their organizations; if not, progress could be slow or nonexistent.

Conflict

(l) A consortium can be viewed as a new game that requires that rules and member roles be clearly defined.

(2) Mediators can help resolve conflict. A neutral planner can serve this purpose.

(3) When a consensus cannot be reached through employer negotiation, productivity of the planning group may deteriorate. Project planners should be alert to the warning signals of apathy, absences and open hostility, and use mediating skills to identify and resolve the underlying conflict.

[1] Elizabeth L. Morgan and Diane Hawk Spearly, *Child Care Consortiums by Employers: Four Interorganizational Issues to Consider When Developing a Joint Project*. Washington, D.C.: U.S. Department of Health and Human Services, Office of Youth and Families, 1984. (Issued by Austin Child Guidance and Evaluation Center, Texas.)

supporting families and children of employees working in tenant companies:

"Larger companies have been the first to discover the benefits of providing parent-support services. The same benefits can accrue to smaller employers that band together in a consortium to provide similar services. A natural setting for such a consortium is an office or industrial park where many companies, working with park management, can collectively provide these quality services in a cost-effective manner. Park management [at The Prospect Hill Executive Office Park] believes that parent-support services provided by this consortium approach make the park a better place in which to work and assist the companies to improve their performance."[2]

The geographic proximity of organizations is important to successful collaboration if the employees of each organization are to benefit equally from a jointly sponsored program. Consortia in downtown urban areas and in suburban industrial parks are gaining in popularity because of the convenience for closely located employers.

The disadvantages of collaboration occur when success must be shared. If increased public recognition is one of the objectives of involvement, less attention will be focused on

[2] Eleanor T. Nelson, *A Case History: The Consortium Model at Prospect Hill Parents' and Children's Center.* Massachusetts: Prospect Hill Executive Office Park, 1986.

each participating company since the limelight will be shared. If one company spearheaded the effort, it might become known as "the Company X initiative," and other participants may receive less attention. The Northside Child Development Center in Minneapolis was started by 13 companies in 1969. It is usually referred to in the literature as "Control Data's center."

When sharing administrative responsibilities, a company may reduce the amount of staff time spent on the project, but it may also lose some control over program decisions. Often, this trade-off between responsibility and control is not realized until after program implementation.

Another disadvantage of collaboration is the extra time needed to reach final decisions. If each representative must also seek approval from his or her respective company before decisions can be made as a group, the process becomes lengthy.

A related concern is the effects of uneven expertise among consortium members. Some may not—or may not be able to—contribute as much as others. Some companies reported that this resulted in negative feelings and wasted time. The groups will also fluctuate in size. There is a natural attrition due to job changes among members. There also may be requests for participation once the collaboration has received positive recognition and publicity. The success of the project attracts people who may be interested in the results for reasons which may differ from those of the original collabora-

A Consortium Day-Care Center in Downtown Atlanta

In 1983, legal counsel for Rich's Department Store in Atlanta became interested in developing a downtown child-care center. There was the possibility of using space on the eighth floor within the department store, but licensing laws prohibited child-care programs above the ground floor. Rich's called in Corporate Child Care Consultants, Ltd. to find other space and help identify other companies to participate in a downtown center. The Executive Director of Central Atlanta Progress became aware of the initiative and saw the downtown child-care center as furthering the city's goals of rejuvenating the downtown area. His access to Atlanta's corporate CEO's helped bring together representatives from Rich's, Georgia Pacific, and *The Atlanta Journal Constitution.* The participating companies contracted with Corporate Child Care Consultants to locate sites for the child care center and develop preliminary budgets. After six months, the study was completed.

With Rich's donating 8,900 sq. ft. within their department store, it was agreed that the center be located on the ground floor of the store. After this was determined, First Atlanta Bank and The Federal Reserve Bank joined the effort. The five companies incorporated and chose the name "The Downtwon Child Development Center," which eventually opened on December 2, 1985.

There were numerous legal, administrative, financial and programmatic issues to be resolved by the consortium members. Several months were spent developing an agreement which designated financial contributions and determined the responsibilities and obligations of each participating company. An attorney assisted in developing a five year plan and in incorporating the center.

Another question was whether the center should be considered a benefit or a service? There were advantages and disadvantages to each arrangement. It was eventually decided that because parents would be paying a portion of the fees, it would be more appropriate to consider the center a service. Each company contributed an equal amount to cover start-up costs, although Rich's share was reduced because they were donating space for the center. A commitment was made by each of the five companies to contribute annually to the center, which was established on a nonprofit basis so that companies, as well as other funding sources, could make additional contributions to the program.

The fees were established at $75 per week for infants and $55 for children ages two to five. In September, 1986, these fees were raised to $80 for infants and $60 for two to five year olds. However, if the rent and all other donated

tors. The unevenness of the group's goals and involvement may make collaborating more difficult.

Structure of Collaborative Efforts

Consortium planning and administration may be informal or highly structured. The ongoing responsibilities of representatives to the consortium also vary. There is usually a coordinator, who initiated the idea and who is responsible for calling meetings, keeping minutes, and motivating the group to action. The coordinator may be a corporate representative, the developer of an industrial park, or the social service or government agency seeking employer involvement. A Vice President of the BankAmerica Foundation is the coordinator for California's Child Care Initiative Project.

Graphic Controls in Buffalo, New York mobilized 20 companies in the community to initiate a downtown center. The information it had collected during an investigation into the possibility of establishing a day-care center for its employees was useful to the other employers, and the company is playing a key role in the development of a downtown center. The Burbank School District played the convening role for seven employers in the creation of a child-care center housed in an unused and refurbished public school building. The Academy of Television Arts and Sciences coordinated a child-care center for five of its member TV and radio stations. The Center on Aging at the University of Bridgeport coordinated an eldercare program for four companies in the Bridgeport, Connecticut area.

The planning process is often facilitated by a task force that assumes responsibility for major decisions. A company representative or a United Way leader might chair the task force while volunteers are recruited from other organizations known to have expressed interest in the program under consideration.[3] A sample of consortia from around the country provides the flavor of this diversity in the planning structures and shared decisions.

• In 1982, Herman Miller Company of Holland, Michigan conducted a feasibility study for providing child care. Contact with the local child-care referral agency and other area employers led to a decision to expand the referral service by generating support from local companies. Herman Miller initially underwrote the program and then sponsored a luncheon for 65 companies to advocate for their participation in the program. Initially eight companies became members of the referral service, called Quality Child Care System, and four others joined at a later date. Five of the contributing companies had considered sponsoring a child-care center, but rejected the plan because it was too costly. The membership fee for the referral service was $250 plus one dollar for each employee over 50 employees.

[3] See Kathryn Troy, *Meeting Human Needs: Corporate Programs and Partnerships*. The Conference Board, Report No. 881, 1986.

services were factored in, the tuition costs would be significantly higher. The companies agreed to cover any unforeseen shortfalls. The one thing that consortium members agreed upon was the need for a high quality center and the willingness to pay for it.

Any unforeseen shortfalls would also be split among the companies. The one thing that consortium members agreed upon was the need for a high quality center and the willingness to pay for it.

The eight months before the center opened were very busy for the consultants and representatives from consortium companies. Liability insurance had to be secured. They reviewed bids and hired an architectural firm. A contractor was hired six months before the center opened. The participating companies donated a large amount of goods and services, such as furniture, fixtures, doors, etc. Various vendors to Rich's donated washers and dryers, carpet and padding, and other items.

The director of the center was hired three months before the center opened. She visited each of the companies in order to work with their public relations departments to assure adequate publicity about the center's availability. Pre-enrollment forms were prepared for each company that was assigned 20 slots for its employees. If a company did not use all of its slots, they were made available to the general public. When the center opened in December, 20 children were enrolled, despite its capacity to serve 120 children. By February, there were 47 children. The center reached full capacity in June of 1986.

The consultants who assisted the consortium committee recommend the following:

• Put on the Board of Directors representatives of the companies who are able to make corporate decisions, or have access to high level management.

• Develop several subcommittees on which other company representatives would serve to implement the policies and programs set by the Board.

• Educate members early in the process, perhaps by showing them a day-care center like to one they envision.

• Meet individually with each consortium member to assure that each company representative has an equal opportunity to express their views.

• Keep several slots open to the public to protect the center from under-utilization and to enhance community relations.

• Retain consultants for several hours per month once the program has opened. This permits some continuity of support and a background of knowledge to be available as new staff settle into the program.

In addition to referral counseling, the Quality Child Care System also trained new providers of child-care services, increasing the supply of family day-care homes from 37 to 78 in a two-year period during which employers supported the program. The number of parents receiving referral assistance also increased—from 105 to 721—during the same period. An evaluation of the Holland consortium indicated that public relations, community image, and publicity were the prime motivating factors for company participation. All participating companies expressed high satisfaction with the program except for Parke-Davis, which did not renew its membership after one year due to very limited use of the program by employees.[4]

• The Broadcasters' Child Development Center was created in 1980 by contributions of $7,000 from each of five television and radio stations in Washington, D.C. The National Academy of Television Arts and Sciences (NATAS) organized the effort, and located a church convenient to all contributors where the center would be housed. (The center was later moved to a nearby elementary school building.) The stations do not have any ongoing financial responsibility, although representatives sit on the board of directors and NATAS contributes annually. The center is open to anyone in the broadcast industry.

• Developers Arthur and Eleanor Nelson had a commitment to education before they began building the Prospect Hill Executive Office Park outside Boston. In early 1983, three companies within the park approached management with the idea of creating an on-site, child-care center. An assessment of employees' needs within the 29 tenant companies indicated that a child-care center would be of great interest to a majority of employees who were in their childbearing years and in two-earner families. Architectural designs and cost projections were prepared as planners discussed financial support from tenant companies. It became apparent that companies were not in the position to invest the estimated $150,000 needed for the capital budget.

While plans for a day-care center were postponed, Park management provided support for a resource and referral program, a counseling program for families of school-age children, parent-education seminars, a resource library, and management-information services for employers through seminars, newsletters and consultation. Most of these services are offered through the Prospect Hill Parents' and Children's Center, which opened in 1984 as a non-profit corporation for participating companies and the public. The child-care center, called the Children's Place, serves 45 children and was opened in 1985. Based on the number of employees, the company is charged a membership fee that grants its employees enrollment priority to the Children's Place and the opportunity to participate in the other programs provided by the Parent Resource Center. Fees paid by parents cover most of the expenses for the child-care center, although Park management subsidized the budget during the first year, and continues to subsidize the rental of space. Through the creation of Workplace Connections, Prospect Hills Parents' and Children's Center now serves as a prototype for consultation to corporations and other consortia.

• In 1982, the President of Voit Companies, which manages the Warner Association, met with companies that employ about 15,000 of the 35,000 employees who work in the Warner Center, outside Los Angeles. The intent was to develop three or four issues of importance that the Association could work on together. The four issues that emerged were transportation, security, emergency preparedness, and child care.

Staff responsible for pursuing the child-care issue distributed a questionnaire to 4,000 of the employees working in Warner Center to learn more about their current work situations and family responsibilities. Each of the participating companies appointed a member of the task force that would plan the child-care initiative. A professor of child development from a neighboring university was hired on a part-time basis to advise the task force. They chose to involve another neighboring college and the United Way, acknowledging that the process might take longer with greater involvement. They used the extra time to educate top management about the need for child-care assistance. As one of the planners commented: "The more players involved, the longer the process. It may be little bit more cumbersome, but the strength of that partnership is going to sustain the program over the long haul. What we are creating is a sense of ownership."

After three years of discussion, a child-care center was opened in January, 1987, serving 75 preschoolers. The center, located in an occupational center operated by the Los Angeles Unified School District, is managed by the non-profit Warner Center Institute for Family Development, a cooperative venture between public agencies and private business. Child-care spaces have been apportioned to the participating firms in the Warner Center. The companies provided the startup costs, and parent fees will cover ongoing operating expenses.

• In 1982, the Burbank (California) School District received a grant from the state Department of Education to organize a task force to create a child-care center in an unused school building. The identified stakeholders in the center were the school district, employees, employers and children. The school determined that it would cost $70,000 to renovate the space for a child-care program. The school's early childhood education specialist, on staff because of four other extended day programs run by schools, contacted a nearby hospital and two of the larger companies to determine their interest in contributing to the startup costs. These initial contacts led to the identification of several other peo-

[4] Bonnie Church Pillar, *Holland Area Employer-Sponsored Community Coordinated Child Care: A Case Study.* Michigan: Western Michigan University, 1985, unpublished dissertation.

ple within companies that had already explored several child-care options. A group of seven companies agreed to contribute $10,000 each in exchange for 20 slots in the child-care program for their employees. Another 20 slots were reserved for community residents. Interviews with the seven employers indicate some of their advice to other companies:

(1) *Recognize mutual self-interests among the participants.* The schools were interested in demonstrating the merits of earlier schooling to parents and filling an unused building. The companies were interested in improved public image and recruitment.

(2) *Take advantage of existing resources.* The companies were not willing to build a new building. The available school space cut down on the cost.

(3) *Begin with one committed manager.* The interest of one employer in a community usually means others will participate once a leader is identified.

(4) *A coordinator is essential.* One person should be responsible for setting up the meetings, monitoring the planning process, and negotiating with individual companies. One manager stated: "This person's tenacity must be matched to his or her negotiating skills. It was helpful that this individual (who was in the school system) was neutral to all the companies.

(5) *Make it easy.* One company commented: "The opportunity to contribute to this center fell into our laps and everything was made so painless. We needed to take the risk, but the risk was shared. With the school in charge, we felt we were in safe, competent hands."

Chapter 6
Return on Investment

Managers are justifiably interested in the bottom-line relationship between work and family issues. For some, collection of these data is necessary before approval can be given to conduct research on specific options. In this case, research focuses on the degree to which employees' family concerns affect their work behavior.

In other companies, management requires estimates of how proposed programs will solve the management problems created by family concerns. In the first case, the data show how much the company is *losing by not responding* to family problems. In the second instance, research is focused on how much can be *saved by responding* with a family program. Companies have used both types of data to justify involvement with family concerns at the workplace.

Companies often find the search for data on either of the above dimensions difficult. There is scant research on the subject and much of what exists does not meet strict methodological standards. The difficulty in generating decent research in this area is attributed to:

(1) *The cost of the research.* Reliable data, generated by longitudinal studies, require substantial investments over a long period of time. Research validity requires before- and after-tests to make certain that the changes observed did not occur because of some preexisting or unrelated simultaneous factors. Sound research also requires control groups, to assure that any changes would not have occurred without the program intervention under investigation. Most companies find this research too complicated, invasive or expensive to conduct.

(2) *Simultaneous changes in the company.* Companies with pioneering work-family programs typically provide other supportive benefits and work innovations. As a result, it becomes difficult to attribute positive outcomes to the family program alone.

(3) *Limited program use.* When only a small number of employees use the family program, the overall effect on the company will be small. One firm with 19,000 employees had a voucher program for child care serv-

ing approximately 150 employees per year. They knew that even if each program user's productivity doubled, the final effect on the productivity of the entire company would be negligible.

(4) *Willingness to be studied.* One of the interesting anomalies in the work-family arena is that the majority of companies want to know the effects of family programs before implementation, yet those with such programs do not want to conduct follow-up research. It is rare for a company to take away a benefit, and since most employees seem satisfied with the program, there is no need to spend additional resources on evaluating its effects.

In the absence of sound, empirical research to substantiate the positive effects of work-family programs, corporate testimonials play an important role. Assertions by companies with child-care programs, for instance, are not usually based on any research, but on the subjective impressions of program managers. Though rarely published in research journals or corporate annual reports, these testimonials are often cited in newspapers and magazines. Media coverage is generally oriented towards the positive aspects of the subject so that reports tend to endorse—or even glorify—the company's family support initiative. (See box.) It would be difficult, however, to find a company willing to share "bad news" about a new program or policy.

When the decision-making process begins, most managers seek data on the direct productivity effects of family problems and programs. However, most of the research has produced data on other aspects of work behavior that affect the bottom line, such as recruitment, absenteeism, tardiness, turnover, morale and stress. These factors relate to intermediate changes that must occur if there is to be an increase in productivity.

It seems obvious, for example, that there is a common-sense relationship between predictable attendance and productivity. Reductions in absenteeism, tardiness and turnover lead to increases in productivity. But stress and morale levels do not have such clear effects on productivity. A logical assumption is that too much stress can affect productivity negatively, but one can question whether the reduction of stress will always have a positive effect. Research has shown that a certain amount of stress may, in fact, act as a stimulant. On the other hand, continued tension clearly has adverse health consequences that, in turn, affect productivity.[1]

The effects will also differ depending on the individual involved. For instance, the flexitime schedules of some workers can create stress for other employees who need more order and time rigidity. And working at home may be good for some people while others have a difficult time being productive in such environments.

Morale is sometimes equated with a measure of job satisfaction. The body of research on this point does not confirm a proven relationship between improved morale and increased productivity. One might conclude that doing things to make employees happy does just that—make them happy. What research does show is that increased productivity improves morale, but not necessarily that improved morale increases productivity. In the case of improved morale reported in the research below, it is possible that the family program may have caused a direct improvement in productivity or a reduction in stress and that, in turn, led to an improvement in morale. Some managers also reported the advantage of "humanizing the workplace" with a family initiative.

---

[1] Presentation by Ilene Gochman of International Paper at Work and Family Research Council meeting, sponsored by The Conference Board in Sarasota, Florida, March 28, 1985.

That might make all employees feel good about the company they work for and could lead to a more concerted work effort.

Other benefits often reported by companies center on the less tangible effects on the firm's public image. When the community views the company as a "good employer," it may be more willing to purchase its goods or services. For many years, The Stride Rite Corporation, for instance, has recognized that their Children's Centers are a valuable investment, both for community parents and as an employee benefit. Additionally, the centers have received considerable national recognition and have demonstrated the need for high-quality, affordable, employer-sponsored child care. During the last ten years, Stride Rite has attracted the attention of many companies and has participated in the development of over 50 centers around the country.

Some of those doing research on family issues recognize the limitations of the research on the bottom-line effects of family problems and programs. Even though management requests such data, the research generated tends to be conservative in its claims. Advocates want to avoid overpromising what family-support programs might achieve. They believe it is more important to juxtapose family concerns with other quality-of-work issues. One manager comments: "We have got some pretty tedious jobs in this office, and I can't believe that a child-care program—no matter how helpful it is—will actually make employees work faster or be happier." Ignorance of this aspect of the workplace is exemplified in the marketing strategy adopted by one child-care organi-

---

Selected Media Coverage of Corporate Child-Care Initiatives

Hartzel Z. Lebed (Executive Vice President of CIGNA Corporation), "Child Care at the Office," *Boston Globe*, December 5, 1983.

"Where the [child care] idea has been tried, the results, though difficult to quantify, have been encouraging. Our [CIGNA] managers express their belief that the company's child-care program is yielding major benefits: reduced absenteeism and job turnover, increased employee satisfaction and loyalty."

Sylvia Porter, "Company-Sponsored Day Care Brings Benefits", *The Champaign-Urbana News-Gazette*, August 1, 1982.

"Intermedics Inc...recorded a 23 percent decrease in employee turnover and 15,000 fewer work-hours lost to absenteeism during the [child care] facility's first year of operation. 'The center is more than paying for itself,' notes a company official.

"Wang Laboratories...reported a marked drop in employee turnover and 'very positive effects' on employee morale after establishing its own day-care facility for 150 enrollees in a nearby elementary school. PCA International Inc. . . . states that its day-care center has substan-

tially reduced costs relating to recruitment and turnover—a saving estimated at $50,000 a year."

Andrea Lichota, "Employer-Sponsored Day-Care Centers are Taking Hold," *New York Times*. October 14, 1984.

"In a survey in 1982, Hoffman La Roche found that 78 percent of its employees who used the company day-care center believed their work improved. It also found that tardiness and absenteeism declined...Mrs. Keel Atkins said the convenience and proximity of the center helped to minimize parents' stress and anxiety: 'It's like an invisible umbilical cord.'"

Editorial Opinions section, "You Could Benefit, Too," *Business Insurance*, June 21, 1982.

"Money saved through reduced absenteeism and less employee turnover is linked directly to the availability of day care. We are as skeptical as the next person when someone says the benefit will pay for itself, but that's what many of the employers offering day-care benefits told our correspondent Margaret LeRoux, who probed this issue."

zation. Its ad in a local newspaper reads, *"Personnel problems? Convert boring, low-pay jobs into positions people want to get and keep! Reduce turnover and absenteeism! Improve morale and productivity!—Add child care to your fringe benefit package."*

Within the limitations cited, the research upon which most managers rely is summarized below. While recent research focuses on broad work and family issues, child care has been the focus of the majority of research in the area and major findings on its worth are reported below. The documented effects of flexitime and part-time work are also reviewed.

Research on the Effects of Work and Family Programs

Researchers tend to focus on either the effects of family-support programs initiated by an employer or on the effects of unresolved family problems experienced by employees. In the first case—the evaluation of existing company-sponsored family programs— two basic research strategies have been utilized: (1) national surveys of companies that have already responded to their employees' family needs; or (2) case studies of individual company programs. In the research focused on family problems among employees working for companies that have not addressed their needs, the methodology is essentially one of self-reports from employees. Findings from the two basic types of research studies—examining the effects of either family *programs* or *problems*—and the three methodologies employed are reviewed below.

Effects of Alternative Work Schedules

Reanalyses of University of Michigan panel surveys found that over one-third of employees felt stress due to time demands of work and family responsibilities.[2] While most companies have instituted alternative work schedules as a means to increase output or address commuting and energy problems, there is a presumption that flexitime and part-time work can increase productivity by reducing family strain. It has been assumed that, without research, compressed workweeks tend to be hard on families.

Flexitime

In 14 studies, three of which are considered methodologically sound, the conclusion is that flexitime increases productivity.[3] Other findings from these studies include:

- Perceived improvements in productivity were reported by 48 percent of companies surveyed; 45 percent of the employees surveyed; 22 percent of the supervisors surveyed.

[2] Graham L. Staines and Joseph H. Pleck, *The Impact of Work Schedules on the Family*. Ann Arbor, Michigan: Survey Research Center, Institute for Social Research, The University of Michigan, 1983.

[3] Stanley D. Nollen, "Does Flexitime Improve Productivity?" *Harvard Business Review*. September-October, 1979, pp. 4-8.

- Three quasi-experiments (before and after measures, control groups, etc.) produced "hard data" that showed, on average, a 12-percent increase in output per unit of input.
- The aggregate experience of the studies shows that the chances of a productivity gain from flexitime were between one-third and one-half. The size of the gain was estimated to be between 5 and 15 percent.

Part-time Work

Survey data show that productivity gains were reported by one-quarter to three-fifths of the companies surveyed, and savings were based on reduced labor costs. Such savings could be negated if fringe benefits were provided to part-time employees. The net economic impact of part-time work was that two-thirds to three-quarters of the companies offering part-time work obtained the predicted cost savings. These savings ranged between 10 and 25 percent of costs. These figures, however, are not based on rigorously controlled scientific studies.[4]

These findings are inconclusive for the majority of companies that do not now have alternative work schedules. The different uses of flexible scheduling and their effects on productivity for production workers and salaried employees are unknown. One researcher commented that flexitime has grown slowly in this country because people attempt to document productivity gains when good will alone may be adequate justification.

Effects of Company-Sponsored Child-Care Programs

Three national surveys of companies sponsoring child-care programs are widely quoted in the literature and frequently cited in company task-force reports. The findings from these studies are highlighted below, along with a description of the methodology used. Two other studies are reviewed that used the more empirically based, case-study approach.

National Surveys

Three national studies surveyed employers with child-care programs to determine whether the programs had resulted in improvements in various productivity measures. The majority of respondents were employers with on-site child-care programs, many of them in hospitals. The findings may not be generalizable to other forms of child-care support or to other types of employers. In addition, these reports were not based on actual research conducted within the company, but rather on the impressions of the respondents. Nonetheless, the findings from these studies were among those most frequently used by managers requiring such data.

Table 1 presents the major findings from these studies.

[4] Stanley D. Nollen, "Work Schedules," in Gavriel Salvendy (ed.), *Handbook of Industrial Engineering*. New York: John Wiley & Sons, 1982.

Table 1: Results of Three National Surveys of Employers that Provide Child Care Services

Results of three national surveys of employers that provide child care services

	Perry, 1978*		Magid, 1983†		Burud, et al., 1984††
Survey question	"What, if any, of the following changes are changes that have occurred as a result of having a day care center for employees?" Respondents were given a list of 7 items and were asked to indicate which had been affected by the child care service.	**Survey question**	"Which of the following items do you perceive as having been affected by the child care program?" Respondents were given a list of 16 items and were asked to rank the top 5 items that were *most significantly* affected by the child care service. Each item was then weighted according to the number and order of the rankings and a cumulative rank assigned. (Only positive items were listed, like "recruitment advantage," "less turnover," "lower absenteeism," etc.)	**Survey question**	"Would you say that the child care service has had an effect on any of the following aspects of company operation?" Respondents were given a list of 16 items and were asked to rate the effect of the child care program on each as positive, negative, unknown, or no effect.
Survey sample	58 employers responded, most of which were hospitals with on-site child care centers.	**Survey sample**	204 companies responded.	**Survey sample**	Out of 415 surveys, approximately 178 businesses answered this question. The majority of respondents were employers that sponsor their own day care centers.

Aspects affected	Percentage of employers responding affirmatively	Aspects affected	Cumulative rankings by respondents	Aspects affected	Percentage of employers responding affirmatively
Increased ability to attract employees	88 %	Recruitment advantage	448	Employee morale	90 %
Lower absenteeism	72	Improved employee morale	345	Recruitment	85
Improved employee attitude toward sponsoring organization	65	Lower absentee rates	214	Public relations	85
Favorable publicity because of center	60	Less turnover	211	Employee work satisfaction	83
Lower job turnover rate	57	Attract persons on leave back to work	208	Publicity	80
Improved employee attitude toward work	55	Attract available talented employees	205	Ability to attract new or returning workers	79
Improved community relations	36	Improve employee work satisfaction	170	Employee commitment	73
		Better public relations	154	Turnover	65
		Better community image	137	Employee motivation	63
		Less tardiness	88	Absenteeism	53
		Improve employee motivation	67	Scheduling flexibility	50
		Improve production efficiency	48	Productivity	49
		Availability of temporary help	26	Quality of work force	42
		Tax advantage	14	Equal employment opportunity	40
		Provide equal opportunity employment	13	Quality of products or service	37
		Improved quality of product produced	11	Tardiness	36

*Kathryn Senn Perry, *Employers and Child Care; Establishing Services Through the Workplace* (Washington, D.C.: Women's Bureau, U.S. Department of Labor, 1982).

†Renee Y. Magid, *Child Care Initiatives for Working Parents: Why Employers Get Involved* (New York: American Management Association, 1983).

††Sandra Burud, Pamela R. Aschbacher, and Jacquelyn McCroskey, *Employer-Supported Child Care: Investing in Human Resources* (Boston: Auburn House, 1984).

Source: Prepared by Dana Friedman, " Child Care for Employees' Kids," *Harvard Business Review,* March-April 1986, pp. 28-32.

Despite methodological and sampling limitations, the findings among the three studies are consistent: Among 16 different measures of employee work behaviors, all three studies found that management believed that the child-care program led to improved recruitment, morale and public image in the community. Reduced absenteeism and turnover were among the top five benefits in two of the studies. None of the studies reported any negative effects of child-care provision, although two of the studies did not specifically ask whether negative effects were found.

Empirical Studies of Individual Companies

Only one company has conducted a controlled study using an experimental design. The Northside Child Development Center (created in 1969 by Control Data and 13 other

What Companies Lose By Not Responding To Employees' Family Problems

In an effort to establish a link between family problems and productivity, several researchers surveyed employees in companies that had not yet implemented family-support programs. The findings from this research provide evidence of employee absenteeism, tardiness and stress that, according to employees, result in a loss of productivity. The data suggest that the bottom line may be affected negatively when companies do not address the family needs of their employees. Highlights from five of these studies are reported below:

Dianne S. Burden and Bradley Googins, **Balancing Job and Homelife Study: Summary of Findings.** Published by Boston University School of Social Work, Boston, Massachusetts, 1985.

Data were collected in 1984 on a 24-page questionnaire sent to all employees in three divisions of a large Boston-based corporation—a management setting, a clerical setting, and a blue-collar field setting. Approximately 57 percent of employees (709) responded. The findings of the study related to the workplace impact of family concerns are highlighted below:

- Parent employees, both male and female, spend from 15 to 25 more hours per week on combined work and family responsibilities than do nonparent employees.
- 49 percent of married working mothers report full responsibility for home chores, while only 4 percent of married working fathers report full responsibility.
- Women employees are six times more likely to have to stay home with a sick child (57.1 percent) than are male employees (9.4 percent).
- While at work, over one-third of parent-employees worry about their children always or most of the time.
- The most frequently mentioned sources of job-homelife conflict were: scheduling difficulties, inability to leave problems at work or at home, and job travel.
- Measures of well-being, such as depression and life satisfaction, are most strongly associated with job-family-role strain, not with gender. Men who have increased family responsibilities are as likely as women to have decreased well-being.
- Absenteeism is most strongly associated with decreased health and energy levels. Health and energy, in turn, are associated with the amount of job-family-role strain and hours spent on home chores.
- Over 33 percent of employees felt that the company was not sensitive to the needs of a working person such as themselves. Parent employees, both female and male, felt the company was less sensitive to their needs than nonparents did. They recommended that the company lessen work-family stress by increasing company sensitivity to work-family issues, and by offering more flexible work hours and child-care benefits for parent-employees.

Ellen Galinsky, Diane Hughes, and Mary Beth Shinn, **The Corporate Work and Family Life Study.** Published by Bank Street College of Education, New York, 1983-1986.

In June, 1985, a questionnaire was distributed to two divisions of Merck and Company, Inc. in Rahway, New Jersey, and was returned by 733 employees (53 percent response rate in one division, 50 percent in the other). The study, in progress since 1983, is part of a cross-national research project with counterparts in West Germany, England and Sweden. The major findings are summarized below:

- Approximately one-third of the respondents found it difficult or very difficult to manage their work and family life.
- Among married respondents, 59 percent of women and 47 percent of men experience some or a great deal of interference between work and family life. Parents with children under age six were the most likely to say that work and family conflicted (68 percent of women and 51 percent of men).
- Family conditions accounted for work-family interference for women: age of the youngest child; the husband not doing his share; and the breakdown of child-care arrangements.
- Job conditions explained work-family interferences for fathers, such as autonomy, supervisor relationships, job demands, and job security. For men, having a supervisor who was insensitive to work-family needs resulted in greater stress and more frequent psychosomatic symptoms.

Arthur Emlen and Paul Koren, **Hard to Find and Difficult to Manage: The Effects of Child Care on the Workplace.** Published by Regional Research Institute for Human Services, Portland State University, Portland, Oregon, 1984.

The study is based on a May, 1983 survey of 20,000 employees from 33 companies and agencies in the Portland, Oregon area. The four-page survey was returned by 8,121 employees for a 40 percent response rate. The findings are confirmed by two other surveys on which the Portland

companies) was the focus of a study conducted in 1975 that compared the absenteeism, turnover and productivity rates of 30 employees using the child-care center, 30 employees with other child-care arrangements, and 30 nonparents. The study found significantly lower absenteeism and turnover among the 30 center users when compared to the other groups. (See Table 2.)

A federally funded study, conducted during 1983-1984, tried to implement a control-group study for a variety of different types of child-care programs. (Most of the other research focused on on-site day-care centers.) Various productivity measures were compared for employee-parents and nonparents in companies with on-site centers, voucher programs and resource and referral programs. The more direct form of assistance (i.e. the on-site center) showed the greatest beneficial effects, while resource and referral showed negligi-

researchers cooperated in Washington, D.C. (1982) and in Kansas City, Missouri (1986). The major findings were:

- Fifty-nine percent of the women and 40 percent of the men had difficulty finding child care.
- Thirty-eight percent of the women and 23 percent of the men with children under twelve responded that they had difficulties in combining work and family responsibilities.
- Women with children under 12 years of age missed about 11.7 days of work per year, compared to women with no children (who missed 9.6 days per year). Fathers with children 12 and under missed 9.4 days per year, while childless men missed 7.4 days per year.
- Forty-six percent of mothers using out-of-home care reported child-care stress, compared to 36 percent of fathers with similar arrangements. However, fathers missed as much time as mothers when children were home alone caring for themselves.
- Absenteeism rates were lower for employees relying on care at home by an adult compared to employees using out-of-home care in child-care centers or family day-care homes. The highest absenteeism rates were among parents who relied on children for self-care or sibling care.

John P. Fernandez, **Child Care and Corporate Productivity.** Lexington Books, Massachusetts, 1986.

A total of 7,000 management and crafts employees in five technically-oriented companies located in the Midwest were mailed questionnaires in March, 1984. Findings are based on the responses from 4,971 employees, or 71 percent of the sample. The major findings:

- Among employees with children 18 and under, 77 percent of the women and 73 percent of the men had dealt with family issues during working hours.
- Forty-eight percent of the women and 25 percent of the men had spent unproductive time at work because of child-care issues.
- Forty-five percent of the women, compared to 17 percent of the men, indicated that providing care for a sick child was at least somewhat of a problem.
- Thirty-seven percent of the women (against 16 percent of the men) felt that handling dual roles created stress on the job at least to some extent.
- Instances of missed days at work, tardiness, leaving work early, and dealing with family issues during working hours were strongly related to employees' difficulties in coping with child care and handling dual family-work roles.

- Three-fourths of the women surveyed (76 percent) and more than half of the men (58 percent) believed that increased corporate involvement in child care would increase productivity.
- Forty-seven percent of the women with children under five years old, 12 percent of the men with children under age two, and 9 percent of the men with children 2-5 years old had considered quitting their jobs because of child-care problems.
- Forty-six percent of all mothers and 24 percent of all fathers with children under five had experienced six or more different types of child-care problems, including a sick child, overnight travel, loss of the child-care provider, evening care, selecting the best care, finding quality care, paying for care, transportation, and so on.

The Travelers Employee Caregiver Survey. Published by The Travelers Companies, Hartford, Connecticut, June, 1985.

In June, 1985, a form was sent to 1,412 employees, representing a 20-percent sample of Travelers Home Office employees aged 30 or older. Fifty-two percent of the sample (739 employees) returned the form and 28 percent of this group indicated they were currently providing care for a relative or friend aged 55 or older. Of those providing care, 136 (71 percent) completed the detailed survey that was mailed to them. The survey indicated that:

- Four in ten care-givers manage the elderly person's finances and nearly three in ten provide direct financial support.
- The average duration of time that care-givers have been providing care to elderly relatives or friends is five and one-half years.
- Employees reported providing an average of 10.2 hours per week of care for an older relative. For female employees (who were much more likely to be primary care-givers), the average amount of time spent per week was 16.1 hours, whereas males reported an average of 5.3 hours per week spent in providing care.
- When asked whether care-giving responsibilities interfere with social and emotional needs and family responsibilities, 20 percent of care-givers felt that the responsibilities interfered frequently or most of the time. Eighteen percent of the care-givers have not had a vacation away from care-giving responsibilities for more than two years.

Table 2: A Day-Care Center's Effect on Turnover and Absenteeism[1]

Sample Groups	Turnover Rate	Absenteeism Rate
Users of company-sponsored day-care center	1.77	4.40
Users of other child-care programs in the community	6.30	6.02
People without preschool children	5.50	5.00

[1] George Milkovich and Luis Gomez, "Day Care and Selected Employee Work Behaviors." *Academy of Management Journal*, March, 1976. (Study of the Northside Child Development Center in Minneapolis; initiated by Control Data and 13 other companies.)

ble gains. The ability of referral programs or voucher systems to yield a return for the company depends on the adequacy of the child-care market. If the programs in the community are unstable and of poor quality, the parent may still face interruptions despite efforts to help them find or pay for care.

Research on Effects of Work and Family Problems

Recent studies have begun to explain how employees balance their work and family responsibilities: how much family members help; what services they use; and how understanding their supervisors are. This research also reveals the prevalence of needs and the family demographics of the employee population—data that the company often lacks, but needs for decision making. In addition to exploring employees' current work-family arrangements, companies also learn how employees' dual roles affect their ability to be productive at work and at home: how much stress is felt; how often they have been absent or late because of family problems. A company can infer from these data where they are losing productive time and effort because of unresolved work-family conflict.

This research is based on wide-scale surveys of employees. One of the most useful features of this strategy is that *all* employees are surveyed—not just those with a particular family concern, such as child care. This permits comparisons among various categories of employees. This research had been conducted as part of multicompany studies in which several employers agreed to distribute the same survey to their employees. Other studies have focused on the responses from a single company, although employees at several company sites may be surveyed. The research may focus on only one family problem, although a growing number of companies have been willing to explore the full range of work-family issues.

Five of these studies are reviewed in the box on pages 41-42. Although focused on various work and family issues, there are some consistent findings:

- A significant portion of employees (ranging from 30-60 percent) find it difficult to manage the dual responsibilities of work and family.

- The interference between work and family responsibilities may be caused by family conditions, such as the age of the child or the adequacy of support services, or may be due to job conditions, such as scheduling or job demands.

- The interferences between work and family responsibilities may affect family stress or personal well-being. It might also affect work performance in terms of absences, lateness or daily interruptions.

- Both male and female employees with dependents (either children or aging relatives) generally experience more strain and work-family conflict than employees without dependents.

- Working mothers experience greater work-family conflict than working fathers. Men, however, are not immune to the negative effects of the dual responsibilities for home and work.

- The job effects of work-family conflict for working mothers is greater than for working fathers. One study provides an explanation of sex differences, suggesting that men's absentism is low *because* women's absenteeism rates are high.[5] Women are the ones who stay out with sick children, leave work for an emergency, and take on the responsibility of looking for child care. They conclude that absentism is not a "women's problem" but, rather, a "family solution." The authors contend that absenteeism need not lead to lost productivity because "modest amounts of employer flexibility in accommodating the inevitable can boost morale and productivity."

- Most employees believe that some support from the company in the form of more flexible work policies or new services would help mitigate some of the conflict between work and family life.

[5] Arthur Emlen and Paul Koren, *Hard to Find and Difficult to Manage: The Effects of Child Care on the Workplace*. Regional Research Institute for Human Services, Portland State University, Portland, Oregon, 1984.

Chapter 7
Analyzing the Data

Decision making for family-support initiatives involves obtaining answers to at least these basic questions:

(1) Should the company respond to family concerns? If so, why?
(2) What direction should the company take to respond to family concerns?
(3) How should the response be implemented?

Answers to these questions provide a company with the rationale for involvement, a program choice, and a strategy for implementing the chosen response to employees' family needs. Companies consult a variety of stakeholders and data sources throughout the decision-making process. The data used by most companies, in varying combinations and frequency, and described in this report, are listed in the accompanying box.

After reviewing the objectives of the research effort, the various data sources are then integrated to get a clear picture of the problem and the extent of corporate responsibility for solving it. Understanding both the problem and, to the degree possible, its causes, is the second step in analysis, managers report. The next question often posed is: Given what we know about the nature of the problem, what needs to be changed? Answers to this question can lead to the identification of broad areas of concern and the basic strategies for addressing them. For instance, do the solutions rest in new community programs, employee services, or benefits? Should work policies or schedules be changed? Should existing policies or programs be managed differently?

Once a list of program ideas is developed, most companies analyze their choices along three dimensions:

(1) *Level of importance.*Decision makers generally assign priority to each of the program ideas under consideration, considering the severity of the problem, the numbers of employees it affects, and the concerns of the company.
(2) *Ease of implementation*. Some solutions require revisions of corporate policy. Others require additional research before the feasibility of the solution can be

determined. For companies anxious to provide some response after research, the tendency is to choose options that can be initiated quickly and inexpensively. Parent-education seminars and changes in leave policies often fall into this category.

(3) *Cost*. It is difficult, if not impossible, to estimate the cost of a family-supportive initiative without knowing the number of potential users, what is already in

---

Data Needs

The following data can provide a company with a rationale for involvement, a list of possible solutions and a strategy for implementing the chosen response. Company priorities will depend on a blend of the factors listed below:

Internal Environment

I. Management Agendas
- Corporate readiness
- Top-management support
- Organizational resources
- Organizational structure
- Mid-management support
- Labor union support
- Return on investment

II. Employee Needs
- Employee attitudes
- Scope of employee needs
- Nature of work-family problems

External Environment

III. Community Activity
- Competitor involvement
- Public attitudes
- Government activity
- Demographic trends
- Consultants, experts
- Community resources and needs
- Program costs

place within the organization, and the availability of support from outside sources. It is possible to make comparative cost estimates for the various programs under consideration.

All family initiatives require some funding. Staff time has to be allocated for designing and implementing new practices. Beyond that, costs can be estimated on a hypothetical basis. The actual cost of developing a response may also be considered in light of potential savings to the company in the form of improved on-the-job behavior. To ascertain the true return on investment, additional funds might have to be spent on evaluating the effectiveness of an implemented initiative. This is a much later step.

At this juncture, many company task forces prepare a written report and an oral presentation to top management that explain the research process and rationale for decisions, and present a set of recommendations. Typically, the following range of outcomes emerged in the companies interviewed:

- *The plan is rejected.* A lack of management awareness or support, and insufficient evidence of the problem and its effects on the company can cause rejection of the proposed plan. This study found few examples of total rejection, particularly when a lengthy research process had been undertaken.
- *The plan for action is postponed.* Other, more pressing, problems in the firm may cause recommendations to be tabled until a more favorable environment exists. During this volatile period of mergers, downsizing and restructuring, postponement is becoming a more common response.
- *A quick, visible solution is accepted.* A limited response is all that is needed, or the company is interested only in appeasing the demands of a vocal pressure group or in demonstrating its concerns for the community. Family issues seem to reemerge when a limited response has been made and companies support the need for a more comprehensive effort.
- *External programs are approved.* The company may not be ready to change internal policies, but may be willing to be generous to community organizations. Looking closely at many well-known corporate initiatives; there is a tendency to solve work-family problems through community affairs or corporate contributions. These initiatives may eventually lead to changes in internal human-resource policies.
- *A recommendation is accepted for a collaborative effort.* The company may decide to pursue the recommendation in partnership with others because it is unable to absorb the costs alone, or it fears that the program might be underutilized. Further negotiations may be required.
- *A pilot program is approved.* The company wants to test the effectiveness of a proposed program on a limited basis before implementing it companywide. Companies that experimented with the limited approach cautioned that the term "pilot project," for many, implies that the initiative will be replicated on a broader scale. Pilot projects require an evaluation to determine their future.

A Thorough Data Analysis: The Du Pont Experience

The range and configuration of choices available often requires an intense period of dialogue, negotiation and analysis. The Child Care Committee of the Du Pont Company was formed in 1985 to examine the subjects of child care and pregnancy-related issues among four major Wilmington, Delaware locations, including corporate office buildings. The committee recognized the complexity of its task and spent one year developing its recommendations. The committee also developed a unique process for analyzing its data.

This committee comprised a cross-section of individuals from various disciplines within several company divisions. The group first defined the parameters of its investigation: (1) regulations and legal ramifications, (2) employees' perceptions, (3) local support systems, and (4) nationwide corporate initiatives. Subcommittees were organized around these four areas and each was responsible for collecting needed data.

Nearly one year after the first meeting of the task force, the group assembled at the Seaview resort in New Jersey for a three-day workshop to analyze the data and finalize recommendations. Committee members report that this strategy facilitated a rich exchange of ideas and reduced the tendency to think in terms of levels and job titles. Everyone participated on a more equal level when, dressed in casual clothes, they met in an informal setting away from the office. Free time was programmed into the agenda to allow for the healthy digestion of an overwhelming amount of information and uninterrupted reflective thought. The workshop was also intended to convey the company's appreciation for the hard work contributed by task-force members.

The agenda for the three-day retreat is described below:

Day 1 (11:00 am—10:00 pm)
a) Everyone was brought up to date with the data base. Each subcommittee summarized its findings. The outside consultant who conducted the employee survey, focus groups, and community analysis also presented a review of all data and a statistical analysis of need. No debate was allowed: Only comments or questions needed for clarification were permitted.

Day 2 (9:00 am—9:00 pm)
a) Continued reporting of facts learned through research.

Otherwise, the project may result in resentment from employee groups who expected an expansion.

- *Multiple recommendations are accepted, to be implemented over time.* Some program ideas require further research; others are deemed untimely. A few companies believe that launching several new initiatives simultaneously might belittle each in the eyes of employees as well as overwhelm the managers responsible for program implementation. Other companies realize they are treading in new waters and, for practical and political reasons, want to proceed slowly. The importance of *incrementalism* was expressed by a decision-making expert almost 20 years ago: "Policy-making is typically a neverending process of successive steps in which continual nibbling is a substitute for a good bite."[1]

- *Multiple recommendations are to be implemented simultaneously.* The company has the resources and expertise to pursue several solutions that address a variety of work-family problems. Most companies realize that no one solution can solve all of the problems faced by every employee. Packaging several company responses can reduce concerns about equity (i.e., avoid offering a program in which only a portion of employees can participate).

Throughout the interviews with companies, questions were posed to managers about the lessons they had learned: If you were to advise another company about to embark on a simi-

lar fact-finding effort, what would you insist that they undertake—and avoid? Five points were mentioned most frequently:

(1) *Get to the top.* As early as possible in the investigation of family issues at the workplace, seek the support and endorsement of senior executives, preferably the president or CEO.

(2) *Define the issues broadly.* Work-family issues embrace more than child care. The more broadly the issue is defined, the larger the employee population that will be affected.

(3) *Be patient.* The average time that companies took from when the idea to support family issues was a gleam in some employee's eye until implementation was about two years. Learning about the issues, garnering support, and developing programs that fit the corporate culture, takes more time than most managers anticipate.

(4) *What works in one company may be doomed in another.* When borrowing ideas from other companies, consideration must be given to the specific needs of the organization, its employees, and the surrounding community. This is true in the use of decision-making aids, such as surveys and task forces, as well as for the specific programs or policies to be implemented.

(5) *Emphasize process over product.* The decision-making may be as important, or more important for sustaining change than the actual policies or programs initiated at the outset.

[1] Charles E. Lindblom, *The Policy-Making Process.* Englewood Cliffs, New Jersey: Prentice Hall, Inc., 1968, p. 25.

---

b) Two-hour break to read, absorb facts, and prepare for debate.

c) Group reviewed the original objectives to make sure the data were complete.

d) Beginning of discussion of conclusions and recommendations. The consultant and company adviser (a senior executive from Du Pont) were excused from the workshop so the Committee could explore all possible solutions.

Day 3 (9:00 am—3:00 pm)

a) Brainstorming on the question: Given what we know, what needs to be changed?

b) Set priorities on recommendations.

c) Using group consensus, the recommendations were narrowed.

Final recommendations were divided between external and internal activities. They included:

External

(1) Du Pont should play a leadership role in the Delaware community, with regard to child-care issues, particularly to encourage other businesses to support community child-care programs.

(2) A child-care resource and referral system was needed for the Wilmington area. United Way had recently reached the same conclusion and a decision was made to contribute an initial $35,000 in start-up funds to establish the new service.

Internal

(1) Insure worksite consistency in disablility administration.

(2) Adopt "return to work" options for new mothers to ease the transition from childbirth to full-time employment.

(3) Educate workforce regarding child-care policies and issues.

A preliminary report was prepared and submitted to Du Pont's Affirmative Action Committee that chartered the study. Chairing that committee is a top official in the company with the authority to accept the recommendations. With support from the Affirmative Action Committee, all recommendations were accepted as presented.

In recognition of the work of the task force, members were subsequently invited to review their recommendations with the Du Pont Executive Committee.

A Time Line for Decision-Making: The Honeywell Story

Honeywell, Inc., is a company headquartered in Minneapolis, Minnesota, and is generally thought of as one of the more progressive companies in the work-family arena. The company has changed internal policies and programs and has supported a variety of community-based organizations that provide family assistance. Management did not approve any of these initiatives without considerable employee input and research. In fact, since 1980, there have been three different work groups focussed on child care and family issues. While change has occurred, company policy is still evolving. Honeywell's decision-making process is illustrative of the time it often takes to marshall all resources and get full support of management for a corporate response to the family needs of employees.

Fall, 1980

A recommendation of the Women's Council was implemented: the hiring of a full-time working-parents coordinator for one year to develop corporate policies that would address work-family concerns.

Winter, 1980

A Women's Council was formed to study the special needs of female employees. A special area of study was child care.

Summer, 1981

A Working Parents Task Force was organized to develop specific recommendations for corporate change. Fourteen recommendations were developed and thirteen of them were implemented over the next four years.

Fall, 1981

Honeywell became a major funder and advisor of a communitywide resource and referral system for child care.

Spring, 1982

A corporatewide flexitime program was implemented, parenting seminars were offered at headquarters, and parenting fairs arranged in several locations.

Winter, 1982

Divisional Working Parent Task Forces were developed, replicating the one convened at the corporate level. Several existed in the Minneapolis area; others were created in Boston and Clearwater, Florida.

1983-1984

Honeywell assumed leadership positios in a number of external activities—offering managerial, technical and financial assistance to community groups. An educational process continued internally as the results of these efforts were shared with management. Work and family seminars were offered to employees on a range of topics.

Fall, 1984

Headquarters developed the Honeywell Working Parent Guide to Child Care. The working-parents coordinator became co-chair of The Conference Board's Work and Family Research Council.

Winter, 1985

Corporate staff, Honeywell researchers and a consultant began developing a research tool for a survey of salaried employees in one division on work and family issues. The survey was distributed, analyzed and presented over a period of one and one-half years.

Spring, 1985

The Residential Division, the largest of Honeywell's divisions, initiated a discount program with three local child-care centers. The program later became available to all Honeywell employees.

Winter, 1986

A flexible benefits plan was initiated, including a dependent-care options for salaried employees.

Spring, 1986

The vice president for public affairs served on the Attorney General's Statewide Task Force on Child Abuse.

Summer, 1986

A Work and Family Task Team was created with participation from higher-level managers than had served on previous task forces. Chaired by a general manager and senior vice president, this 16-member team made recommendations early in 1987.

Spring, 1987

Work and Family Task Team document was released with five recommendations on: child care; total time-off policy; supervisory and employee seminars; and senior management support and sensitivity.

****

In summary, the provision of family-support programs and the development of policies that accommodate family needs is becoming more widely accepted by corporate decision makers. Most major corporations have already investigated their options, and many have actually changed policy or practice.

The efforts of the pioneering firms reported here indicate that the decision-making process can be complex and time consuming. This may be attributed to the number of data sources that must be consulted and the resulting need for a balanced integration of many facts and opinions. The complexity of the decision-making process may also be due to the sensitive nature of the subject matter; the fact that family issues at the workplace is a new concept that departs from traditional business practice. This often requires delicate negotiating by the manager who chooses to champion this issue.

Those who have managed the decision-making process for developing family-support benefits attest to the need for both research skills and political aplomb. In addition to the intended benefits that accrued from the specific programs generated by the effort, the process also helped to create a workplace environment that engendered sustained support for employees in their efforts to remain productive at work and at home.

M

P